Pieces of Mary

A HARROWING STORY OF MENTAL ILLNESS AND A JOURNEY
TO RECOVERY THROUGH A BROKEN SYSTEM OF CARE

Pieces of Mary

MARY JORDAN, MS, BSN, RN

Charleston, SC
www.PalmettoPublishing.com

Pieces of Mary

First Edition

Paperback ISBN: 979-8-88590-906-8

eBook ISBN: 979-8-88590-907-5

In keeping with the 11th Tradition of Alcoholics Anonymous to protect my identity as a recovering alcoholic I am writing under a pen name.

DEDICATION

My writing of this book could not have been accomplished without the caring and love from Lara, my daughter, Conrad, my son-in-law, and my three grandsons, Jose, Anthony, and Gregory.

Words cannot convey how you all have enriched my life in so many ways. You have all taught me how to be a better person.

I LOVE YOU ALL TO THE MOON AND BACK!

CONTENTS

PART TWO

A SPECIAL THANKS

I want to thank my family, friends, and
mentors who have touched my life in many
ways. You all have changed my life one
day at a time. I will always be grateful.

ANOTHER SPECIAL THANKS

Thanks to the registered nurses who have participated in my Nurse Support Groups since 1997. I am blessed and honored to have played a role in their recovery. Witnessing their courage and continuous self-honesty as they progress in their journey fills me with eternal love and gratitude.

ACKNOWLEDGMENTS

I want to acknowledge with gratitude my editor, Sara Johnson of Chicago, Illinois. Her talent for correcting, condensing, and modifying my words adds life to my story. Her way of looking at each sentence and making sure it was well designed and served its purpose was but one of her well-polished editing skills.

I can't express enough thanks for the creative guidance and wisdom she added to my memoir. She continuously inspired me to speak my truth. I sincerely appreciate her talent and intelligent contributions to getting my story to publication.

CHAPTER 1

Losing My Mind

June 18th, 2018

How did I get here? How did I get to this point—how did I let it get this detrimental?

When did this destructive eclipse begin? How did it take over my entire being, my entire existence?

Oh God, help me! Help me see beyond the darkness, to see my accomplishments, my contributions, my successes, and my life. Please take away this darkness. Please, God! Please take away the darkness...

IT'S BEEN ANOTHER LONG night, one of many this past week. I can't sleep. My mind has been racing with unintelligible thoughts. This has been happening frequently lately, night after sleepless night I'm left alone with no solution.

After hours of laying, stirring sleepless in bed, I surrender the night over to my television set. I sit up, and slowly take in a deep breath, absorbing the dark room around me. To my left, I look out a window. It's still dark outside. It must be early in the morning.

I pull the blankets off my lap to free myself from their hold. I scoot to the edge of the bed and shift my legs off the right side. My feet pat the floor as I search for my slippers in the dark. It's not difficult to find

them since my eyes have long adjusted to the darkness. I stand up, shuffling over to my bedroom door.
I make my way to the living room, dragging one foot
behind the other, creating a shuffling sound that fol-
lows me down the hall.

"shhhuh, shhh, shhh...."

It sounded as though my feet were shushing my
thoughts. It did not work, however. My mind was as
turbulent as ever. This prompted me to pick up my
pace just a bit so I could reach my TV all the sooner.

—Why me? Why now? Oh God, make it all stop!

I turn round the corner to my left as I exit the
hallway. I maneuver past my coffee table to the couch
and drop myself onto its cushions. I seep into the
sofa, feeling heavier than ever as my burdensome
thoughts weigh me down.

Click.

The TV lit up with bright colors, blinding me momentarily. My stomach let out a growl as my pupils dilate to accommodate the newfound light.

Pictures flashed across the screen, and there I sat, absent-mindedly watching, waiting for my thoughts to clear—for something to get better. Before I knew it, the rising sun lit the living room.

The living room is the largest room in the house. It holds a large couch with two stuffed chairs on either side and the television in the center of the far wall. There are many windows in this room, each with its own shutters. The shutters remain open, which makes this room bright during the day. There are many pictures in this room as well. As the sun continues to rise, I glance around at all the photos I've collected throughout the years.

Most of them are family pictures. One of my most cherished photos was taken when I was about four years old. It is one of the only pictures I have of myself as a child. It was taken by the local newspaper after an apartment next to ours had burned down. The picture was so old that the only part which remained was of my oldest brother and me. We're only two out of eleven siblings. I had messy brown hair, mismatched shirt and shorts, and a forced smile in the photo.

Along with this photo, I have pictures from when I was a young nurse in nursing school, from when I was engaged, pictures of my beautiful daughter, and many of my grandchildren.

My eyes land on one of the most recent photos, one of me on my 76th birthday surrounded by my family. We were all wearing color-coordinated sweaters. I hired a professional photographer for the photos and got my hair done at the salon just for the occasion.

I looked so happy then. My gray hair was done back with my bangs peeking out. I seemed very put-together. I was wearing elegant pearl earrings and a blue turtleneck. I did my makeup in a way that made my eyes shine bright, and I had on the biggest smile. I looked at the photo but could not connect to that person and the others in the picture. I was in and out of emotional numbness, unable to feel the joy I once had.

A loud growl erupted from my stomach, interrupting my gaze. My hunger, being too strong to ignore, forced me to dig myself out from my cavern on the couch and head to the kitchen.

On my way there, I passed a mirror hung on the wall. Looking at my reflection, I hardly recognized myself; messy, disheveled hair, dark eyes with deep bags, and an expressionless face. I looked down at my clothes—white pajamas with red roses all over—which were now stained with food from wearing them every day for the past week.

My appearance was a bit jarring. I'm used to seeing myself as clean and neat, as I was in the birthday photo.

I felt a sharp pinch in my stomach. My body was demanding food. I pull my gaze from the mirror and drag myself to the kitchen.

In the kitchen, a mountain of dishes sat in the sink—pots, pans, plates, bowls, all the works. The pile of dishes reminded me of the accumulation of dirty laundry I had in my laundry room. I can't remember the last time I did any cleaning... I mentally shrug and make my way to the fridge.

Cold air spills out onto my arms as I open the refrigerator doors, causing goosebumps to form. With a shiver, I looked at all the empty shelves which once held milk, eggs, bacon, yogurt, fruits, and orange juice. I reached in and pulled out the only thing I had a taste for lately: jelly.

I grabbed the peanut butter and bread I had left out on the counter from the last time I made myself a sandwich. The dirty butter knife I had used was also left on the counter. I threw it in the sink and grabbed a new one from my silverware drawer.

I made a peanut butter and jelly sandwich and took it back with me to the living room, and, once there, I noticed my phone on the coffee table light up. I lowered myself back onto the couch, set my plate down, and grabbed my phone.

It was a text from a friend that read:

"Hi Mary, I haven't seen you in a while. Hope you're doing well! Can we expect to see you at the AA meeting this week? Let me know!"

I exited the text app and went to look at my missed calls. Seven missed calls from family, three from friends, and a couple of voicemails from my daughter. I turned my phone off and put it back on the coffee table.

I picked up my sandwich and took a small bite. The peanut butter felt like paste in my mouth, and the jelly didn't help it go down any smoother. As I struggled to eat my meal, I continued watching TV.

❖   ❖   ❖

Bzzzz

Bzzzzz

The sound of my phone buzzing broke my attention away from the TV. I looked at the caller ID to see the name 'John' flash across the screen. John was my eldest brother, and we've always been very close, so it's not unusual for him to check on me.

I hesitantly picked up the phone.

"Hello?"

"Hi Mary, it's John.

"Hi, John."

"How have you been?"

"I'm ok."

"That's it, just ok?"

"Yup."

"It's been a while since I've heard from you. What have you been up to?"

"Not much... How are you and Jane?"

"I'm good, I've been good. Jane's been good too. Not much has changed since our last call. I'm still playing golf, and we're both doing well."

"That's nice. Thanks for the call, John, but I gotta get going."

"That soon? Well, alright. Gimme a call if you need anything, alright, Mary?"

"Yeah, ok. Bye, love you."

"Love you too."

I took a deep breath once the call had ended. I felt a rush of mixed emotions hit me all at once.

Should I have told him something? No, no. Definitely not. But what if I get worse? Oh, I'll just be a burden to him. What can he do anyway?

My thoughts constantly raced back and forth like this, not just with the call but with everything. I rubbed my temples in an attempt to relieve my mind.

I turned my head up and looked around for the first time in hours, and to my surprise, it was already dark out.

Where did the time go?

I got up from the couch to head to bed, fearing another sleepless night. When I got to my room, I crawled into bed and lay there, paralyzed. There's no distracting me from my thoughts now.

❖   ❖   ❖

June 19th, 2018

I HAVEN'T BEEN ABLE to stop the tears from coming. Endless tears stream down my face. It's dark again. The darkness of my room found a way to infiltrate my skin somehow. I felt it heavily in my chest. It hurt, the weight of the darkness. I thought it would help if I put a light on. I turned on the light in my bedroom, and still, the darkness prevailed. It filled my head.

What is happening? Why isn't my medication working?

I turned towards my bedside table, and my eyes landed on the bottles of antidepressants and sleeping pills that sat atop it.

It's that easy, Mary. It's the only way to get out of this misery. You'd be doing yourself a favor, you know.

I snapped my gaze away from the medications and rushed to my bedside. I got on my hands and knees, laced my fingers together, and began to pray.

"God help me! My thoughts are terrifying me. I'm so afraid. Don't let these thoughts control me.

They're telling me to do something I've never imagined before...."

I don't want to do it in my own house.

Go to the casino nearby—you have a free room there just waiting for you to book it.

I can't do it in my own house. This house I've loved all these years has always been my safe haven. Why isn't it protecting me now?

The casino, Mary. Do it there. Save your family the trouble of finding you....

"God, please, help me! I don't want to leave such a loathsome legacy to my daughter. I can't do that to my family. Lord willing, lift this darkness. Get me through the night. God help me!"

There's no way out. You know that.

I had been on my knees most of the night, praying for help. My knees ached from kneeling for so long, but my achy pain was the least of my troubles. I needed help desperately.

The walls of my room moved closer and closer. I was trapped. Tonight, my cherished home has become part of my dark prison.

CHAPTER 2

Seeking Help

I DON'T KNOW EXACTLY when my life started to fall apart, but it was at least six months ago. Six months ago, I began neglecting my personal obligations and responsibilities to others and started to isolate myself. I've been stuck like this for too long. It's time for a change. It's time to get help.

In my desperate state, I managed to make my way into the living room, where I had left my phone the night prior. I called the one person I knew had the knowledge to help me: my psychiatrist.

As the phone rang, I tried to regain some composure, but it was no use.

His secretary answered after a few rings, "Hello, this is Dr. Patterson's office. How may I help you?"

"This is Mary Jordan... I need to speak with Dr. Patterson right away. I'm in terrible shape."

"Oh, Mary. Is everything ok? W-wait one moment, I'll put him on." A wave of relief and impending fear hit me as she put me on hold. Relief because I finally found the courage to seek help. Fear because now I have to *tell* someone about what's been happening in my life. I must admit that there is a genuine issue at hand which has been debilitating me for months.

"Hi, Mary? This is Dr. Patterson. What's going on?"

"Dr, I'm in trouble."

"What kind of trouble?"

"I think I'm suicidal."

The silence that followed that statement felt like an eternity. I could feel my heart pounding to break free from my chest. I can't believe it had come to this, that those words had just come out of my mouth. Vocalizing it out loud for the first time made my situation real. It made it tangible. It's as if, somehow, those six months of slipping hadn't actually happened. It was all just a figment of my imagination until I said aloud that I was suicidal.

My psychiatrist advised me to immediately go to the nearest emergency room with a psychiatric assessment team. I agreed, we quickly said our goodbyes, and I began getting ready to go.

It was already daylight by the time I hung up with the doctor. I ran to my room and grabbed the first set of clothes I laid my eyes on—a change of pre-worn clothes I picked up from the floor. I quickly changed, got myself ready, and began looking for my keys.

Where could they be?

It had been weeks since I last left my house, so it had also been weeks since I used my car. There was no telling where I left them. I searched and searched. I tore apart the bedroom, the living room, and the kitchen. It was no use.

God, you're so useless, Mary. You can't keep anything straight. Look at this place. Look at the mess you've made. It's all your fault. There's no point getting help, you'd just be wasting their time.

My last hope was the car itself. I took a deep breath and let out a heavy sigh, and with that, I marched to the garage.

I opened the door to the garage and switched on a light. Stepping into the garage, I approached my car in front of me, cupped my hands around my face, and peered through the driver's seat window. Sure enough, my keys were sitting on the passenger's seat of the car.

Finally!

I ran back inside, grabbed my purse, and took off. It was about a 30-minute drive from my house to the nearest emergency room. My psychiatrist was the former medical director of the psychiatric unit of this hospital. I hoped he could pull some strings and have me admitted close to home. At least, that's what I was expecting to happen.

The drive was a challenging one. My mind was racing faster than before, and my mental state affected me physically, causing my whole body to shake.

Do I want to do this?

Am I ready to do this?

For my safety and everyone else's on the road, I stayed in the right lane throughout the drive, making sure to drive cautiously.

Oh God, please give me some courage!

Tears began filling my eyes, streaming down my face, and falling onto my lap. I kept wiping them away, trying to keep my vision from blurring, but they kept coming.

❖   ❖   ❖

I ARRIVED AT THE hospital, still shaking and crying as I pulled into the parking lot. When I finally parked my car, I sat for a long while working up the courage to go in. As a registered nurse, I knew what to expect.

Am I doing the right thing?

I knew about the Health and Safety Code 5150 commitment.

Maybe I'm exaggerating. Maybe it's not that bad. Maybe I just need to go home and get a good night's sleep. Maybe I'm not broken after all.

I knew what was going to happen.

CHAPTER 3

BROKEN

I SAT IN MY car, unable to move. My arms were outstretched, hands gripping the steering wheel with the engine still running. I couldn't bring myself to reach for the keys to turn off the car. I tried to keep a steady breathing pattern to avoid hyperventilating. I breathed in and out quickly, "huh-hah, huh-hah."

The tears kept flowing, I couldn't stop them. At this point, it seemed as though I'd lost control over every part of my life.

My hands began to shake even more than they had previously, and my grip only tightened to fight away any unintentional movements.

Here I am, about to turn myself in. I'm surrendering myself to the authorities.

Jesus. What an utter failure.

Now, faced with the reality of months of increased sadness and gloom with no relief, I was still torn. All my years as a nurse had suddenly disappeared. I had no idea what to do or how I could help myself; all I knew was I *needed* to seek external help. I had to concede to my innermost self that my mind was no longer reliable. My illness forced me to hand myself over to the mental healthcare world, where I would have no say in the treatment or the outcome. I must yield to the power and control outside myself, and I could only pray they had my best interest in mind.

The reality of my deteriorating mental health was at the forefront of my mind. I desperately wanted to be fixed.

I finally turned off my car.

"God, grant me the serenity to accept the things I cannot change...."

I began to recite the Serenity Prayer to build up the courage I needed to head inside.

"...the courage to change the things I can, and the wisdom to know the difference...."

Once I finished the prayer, I opened the door, exited my car, and walked to the emergency room entrance. A part of me knew it was time to admit that *I was broken.*

As I went into the emergency room, I realized I had been working with my psychiatrist closely for the past six months. I had a new diagnosis and medications, yet nothing worked. I wasn't any better.

At the age of 73, my longtime psychiatrist, who had been treating me for major clinical depression, mentioned the term 'bipolar' as a possible diagnosis. At the time, I shuddered and quickly joked, "I'd rather be bicoastal or bilingual but not bipolar." I had been treated for clinical depression for 33 years, somehow a more acceptable diagnosis. In society's eyes, a bipolar diagnosis had a more negative and devastating reputation. When people commented about bipolar, it was always with disdain and pity. I was in high denial about bipolar, also known as manic depression, as my new diagnosis. I refused to believe I was *that* sick. I declared it to be a false diagnosis. I not only dismissed it, but I ultimately rejected the notion. I wanted a more socially acceptable and familiar diagnosis like depression.

But the reality now is that I am much worse. I've steadily been losing ground, and I'm sinking fast. My mind always races; my thoughts are out of control—

hectic and repetitive. I've been trying to be part of the 'fix me project,' and nothing was working...

What did I do wrong to cause this? How could I have prevented it?

I entered the hospital emergency room. Upon entry, the luminosity from the bright lights was blinding. I raised my right hand, shielding my eyes for a moment to allow them time to adjust. My eyes were already so irritated from all the crying and wiping of tears. I could *feel* the red around my eyes as yet another irritant attacked them. Once I regained vision, I went to the front desk to check-in.

After checking in, I made my way to one of the many chairs they had in the waiting area. I looked around, taking in my surroundings. The waiting room was a decent size. It would probably fit anywhere from 30 to 40 patients at a time. The color scheme was gray and white; the tile, walls, and chairs were identical. It looked clean. Clean with bright overhead lights, and yet somehow, it was all so *dull*. Perhaps it was me, perhaps I was projecting, but this stale environment made me a bit uneasy.

Would they be able to help me here? Am I safe?

It didn't feel like it. I looked to the clerical staff members, who were all very busy interviewing and screening patients. I then began to look at everyone else around me, at all the patients. I felt my brain shift gears, and I started trying to diagnose each person. The nurse in me wondered why they were all here.

A woman in a red shirt was sitting across from me to my right. She was holding her stomach lightly with her legs outstretched.

Maybe she's pregnant. She could be having complications.

A moment later, a tall gentleman approached, holding a young boy. The boy looked to be about four years old, maybe a bit older. They had come from the direction of the restrooms. The little boy looked terrible, his face was pale, and his eyes were sunken. His little body lay limp in the gentleman's arms.

Oh, they're here for him. Their son must have some illness. So maybe she's not pregnant after all.

I wonder if they're all here for physical ailments. Am I the only one here for mental troubles?

I don't know how long it was before they called my name, but I was emotionally numb by the time they called me. I was no longer able to react normally to my current situation. I had shut down.

"Mary Jordan." The clerk called out.

I got up and went to the cubicle where the clerk was busy typing on the computer. She never looked

up as I answered all the usual questions: name, birthday, address, insurance, etc.

Then, the clerk asked if I was suicidal.

"I wouldn't mind not waking up." It was the first
time I admitted it to another person *in the flesh.*

Amazingly enough, there was a calmness about
that possibility, the possibility of ending my emotional pain. I didn't want to die, but the pain was so
intense that it overpowered my desire to live.

Based on my answer, I was placed in a wheelchair and escorted through the swinging doors to the
back nurse's station. I recognized the nurse's station.
The narrow corridor was lined with many doors and
led to an open area. The area had a long counter with
computers, telephones, and lights. Like the admission area, everyone was very busy on telephones and
computers. They were all racing around like a frenzy
of ants scurrying to get their work done and to move
on to the next thing.

A staff member escorted me to the bathroom. They told me I was to undress and put all my belongings in a plastic bag. I was given a pair of hospital pajamas to wear in place of my clothes. At this time, all my belongings were taken away, including my phone.

I realized I had never called or texted anyone to let them know what was happening. It had all been so humiliating. I felt like a complete failure. Handing over my phone, I knew I was giving away my only outlet to the outside world, to my friends and family. With a slight hesitation, I handed it over.

Within 20 minutes of admission, a medical doctor saw me to provide medical clearance. Upon his recommendation, I was scheduled for evaluation by a psychiatric nurse. This is a routine procedure for all patients who are to be admitted to the ER hospital. It's an authorization from an evaluating medical doctor on whether or not a patient is deemed healthy enough to be transferred to a psychiatric hospital.

After I was medically cleared, I was placed again on a stretcher in the emergency room hallway. They laid me down and tightened a strap across my torso. The strap was probably meant to keep me from falling, but all it did was make me feel trapped. I felt tied down, restrained.

No one said anything to me, and I was too afraid to ask. I felt unsafe and so alone. I turned myself in for my own safety, yet I didn't feel safe.

When will I get help?

Why is no one paying attention?

Have I made the right decision to come here?

The nurse's station was busy and noisy, with many people coming and going. Staff was constantly clicking away on computers, phones were ringing off the wall, and patient call lights were buzzing one on top of the other. As if that weren't hectic enough, endless pages were coming from the overhead PA system.

The corridor lights were again very bright. They proved to be the only light source, as there were no windows. Time passed, and everyone continued. Patients and staff came and went. I wasn't sure what time it was or how long I'd been in the ER. And with no windows, there was no way to tell the general time of day. All I could do to distract myself from my pain was to preoccupy my mind with other means. Laying alone in a stretcher with nothing to do, it was challenging to find a sufficient distraction.

I tapped into my internal nurse once again. The nurse in me wondered about the logistics of the hospital:

What's the staffing ratio like today?

How many patients per nurse? They're prob-ably understaffed. That's a typical pattern in the acute care environment. Nurses have to get used to it; they do the extra work that's required.

What felt like hours later, the psychiatric nurse finally came over to evaluate me. I lay there in the hall while he asked me a series of questions about my mental state. It was humiliating to admit my issues out loud in a public corridor. Part of me wanted to lie and say I was fine so I could get out of there and go home. However, I did not lie; I was honest and forthcoming about all the mental issues I had been struggling with. After our interview, he informed me I would be placed on a 5150 hold as a danger to my-self. He then left without offering any other informa-tion.

During my time on the stretcher, no one came to offer me support, comfort, a calm remark, or reas-surance. Everyone was flitting about. When I finally found the courage to ask what would happen to me, they told me, "We're looking for a bed for you." Familiar with the local hospitals, I assumed they were waiting for a discharge from one of three local psychiatric hospitals. Feeling like a castaway, I became even more alert to my environment. Had I made the right decision coming to the ER after all?

I felt hopeless and lost in the system. My despair heightened as I remained on the stretcher in the corridor. Not knowing what was going to happen next, I was nervous about the uncertainty that lay ahead. With so little information about my care and treatment, I remained fearful and alone the rest of the night.

CHAPTER 4

A Long Scary Ride in the Middle of the Night

THE AFTERNOON SLOWLY PASSED into the evening. I finally noticed a small clock on the wall across from the nurse's station, so, despite there being no windows, I could keep track of the time of day. I watched as each minute passed.

At 8:11 pm, I was allowed to call my daughter. By this time, I'd been told I was being held on a 5150 commitment. I told her they were looking for a bed for me, but I failed to mention the 5150 commitment.

A 5150 commitment is an involuntary 72-hour hospitalization when a person is deemed a danger to others or themselves, thus they must be held for psychiatric evaluation. If at the end of the 72-hour hold the person still meets the criteria of being dangerous, the attending psychiatrist can file for a W&I 5250 certification for up to 14 more days of intensive psychiatric treatment.[1]

I had never experienced losing my rights for my own protection. Throughout the night and into the early morning hours, I was still on that same stretcher in the public corridor across from the nurse's station.

I'd been at the ER since 3:03 pm. Finally, at 2:49 am, a staff member came to me with an update. I had been waiting there, laying on the stretcher for almost *12 hours*.

Up until now, I thought finding a bed for me meant one in a local psychiatric hospital. That was until the staff member gave me some surprising news:

"Mary Jordan? We found a bed for you. The ambulance will be here in a short while."

"Oh good, where am I going?"

"Santa Rosa."

"Santa Rosa? But isn't that like... what, 100 miles away? I wanted a local bed."

"We don't have one that's local."

"But I don't want to go 100 miles away."

"You don't have a choice."

My body froze as the reality of the situation set in. I had no say. I felt like a frightened child. My thoughts all jolted to a halt. Unable to form a coherent thought, all I could do was feel. And I felt a lot. I felt the walls of the corridor close in on me. I felt the ceiling cave in, and the walls crash in towards me. Everything felt suddenly cramped. I couldn't move, I could hardly remember to breathe. I was frightened and panicked. As if I weren't scared before, *now* I had to travel 100 miles to get help. What if they can't help me? I desperately wanted someone there to reassure me. But still, no one was with me. I was all alone.

It had never occurred to me that I wouldn't be in one of the local hospitals. Instead, I was being sent to the middle of nowhere to a hospital I'd never heard of, where I knew no one at *three* in the morning!

Within a few minutes, two men arrived and moved me to another stretcher. The nurse handed them a written report, and they wheeled me down the corridor into another, weaving through the heavy traffic of the ER.

A 5150 patient can be transferred anywhere without consideration of the distance from home. Hence, I was to be transferred to a hospital over 100 miles away.

On my way to the ambulance, I realized I couldn't recall any of the names or faces of the staff from the ER. The nurse in me was very much bothered by this because I had always been excellent with names. Lacking this skill meant that something was very wrong. I was so mentally debilitated that I sought safety in every facet. Knowing the names of the nurses and staff taking care of me would help me feel safer and more connected to them. The fact that I couldn't remember their names showed how terrified I was. I was in survival mode.

A 5150 is a serious step. I knew I needed hospitalization for my safety, but it was a reality I hoped never to deal with—others making decisions for my well-being because I was incapable. However, I lost that ability when my depression became all-encompassing.

As I was taken away, I again realized that since I was on a 5150 hold, my rights were taken away for my own good. I was no longer safe for myself. And, because of HIPAA (The Health Insurance Portability and Accountability Act), the staff couldn't divulge my whereabouts to anyone—including my daughter. HIPAA was enacted into Federal law to protect all patient information confidentiality.[2] No one knew where I was or where I would be going.

Oh God, would they at least call my daughter?

We reached the ambulance docking site of the ER, where I was loaded into the back of an ambulance. Two men got into the front of the ambulance, and once they were situated, we were off.

The ride to Santa Rosa was frightening. It was the middle of the night, and all I could see out of the ambulance's small back windows was pitch black. The two strangers upfront—one drove while the other sat in the passenger seat—talked only with each other. I could hear the mumbles of their voices, but I couldn't quite make out what they were saying.

The back of the ambulance looked like an emergency room at the hospital. Equipped with all the necessary tools a healthcare professional would need, it had blood pressure equipment, IVs, etc. There was cabinetry with glass doors so the dressings and other supplies inside were visible.

I sat alone in the back, alone with only the darkness of the night and my thoughts.

Oh, God! How did it come to this—me, a highly functioning and contributing woman, in the back of an ambulance on the way to a locked facility?

I was in a place of self-harm. Not because I wanted to be, but because it had become a viable option in my deep, dark depression. It was a realistic solution to end the pain of penetrating sadness. I'd never before felt suicide as a solution; it was such a powerful force.

The thought passed through my mind that not one family member knew where I was going. My fear had gotten the best of me. It caused my mind to wander to areas and notions that were illogical and senseless.

I bet these guys don't even work with the hospital.

What? That's impossible.

No, it's not. They know how fragile, how vulnerable you are. They know no one knows where you are.

That can't be true.

They're not driving you to the hospital. They're taking you somewhere else...

Irrational thoughts circled my mind the entire two-hour drive to the Santa Rosa Hospital.

CHAPTER 5

All Alone and Far from Home

WE ARRIVED AT THE Santa Rosa Hospital at five in the morning. Once the ambulance backed into the docking area of the hospital, the two men got out and made their way around to the back. They opened the back doors and pulled me out on my stretcher. I was exhausted at this point—I had been awake for the past 24 hours with very little to eat.

I was not given a chance to get up; instead, the two men wheeled me into the hospital straight to an ER room. Once in the room, I was instructed to get onto the ER bed. I sat up, shifted my legs over the stretcher, stepped my feet onto the ground, and climbed up into the other bed. Usually, hospitals have their patients change out of their regular clothes and into medical gowns. However, I didn't need to undress since I still had on the pajamas from the previous hospital.

I was told to wait for a medical evaluation. Unfamiliar with the admission policy and procedures, I did as I was told. My response to their directions felt mechanical. I felt like a robot following commands.

As I waited, I noticed everything was feeling very distant and foggy. I tried to shake it off, but nothing helped. It had been 14 hours since I could stand and stretch, and the only solace I got was the one moment of standing—getting from the stretcher to the bed. I was stiff all over and *tired*. My lack of sleep only served to intensify my anxiety and confusion.

I had no knowledge of this hospital in Santa Rosa which only added to my unsettling experience. Here I was, at a hospital I had never heard of, 100 miles away from home, in a locked behavioral mental healthcare facility. I couldn't even remember the Serenity Prayer to calm myself. It was a prayer I said many times throughout each day for the past 34 years. All I could manage to get out was "GOD."

Even though my ER record from the first hospital was sent with me, the policy was for me to have another medical clearance history and physical done at this hospital. The MD came and conducted the medical history and physical examination. I cooperated and answered all the questions asked of me.

Once medically cleared for admission, a staff member took me to a two-bedroom quarter. It was a small room. Upon entering the room, immediately to your right was a small bathroom. The bathroom had no doors, only thick rubber curtains. The curtains reminded me of some old saloon doors you'd see in the wild west. Inside the bathroom was a shower (also with rubber curtains), a toilet, a sink, and a make-shift steel mirror that distorted any reflected image. The beds were also on the right, just past the bath-room. There were no pictures on the walls and no natural lighting. Instead, there were fake windows with artificial lights behind them. The fake windows were about three feet wide and six feet tall, and a light shone through thick textured plastic inside. I was left there to wait for my psychiatric evaluation.

While waiting, I ate breakfast since it was about seven in the morning. They served me oatmeal, fruit, and coffee. I finished my meal quickly since I was nearly starving. Not long after, I was informed the doctor was ready to give me a psychiatric evaluation.

On the way to the doctor's office, I took my time to look around and observe my surroundings. The unit was dreary. All the furniture was old, dark, and well-worn. The nurse's station was behind a plexi-glass wall, and the staff was all busy at their comput-ers. None of them looked up. There were no windows in the hallways. The artificial light from the ceiling was glaring. The floor was old and had a gray tinge that stained most of the tiles. As I walked, I could hear my feet drag across the floor.

We arrived at the doctor's office. He was there at his desk waiting for me. I took a seat, and we began the evaluation.

During my talk with the psychiatrist, I exhaled my first deep breath. Everything that led to this point left me wondering if I had come to the right place to get the necessary support to save my life: my hours on the stretcher in the hallway, feeling abandoned by the staff, my terrifying ride to Santa Rosa in the middle of the night, it had all kept me in a state of paralyzing fear. But once I sat down with the psychiatrist, I felt I was finally getting the help I needed and deserved.

The doctor made relevant statements that others had not. He commented on my nursing education accomplishments. He also congratulated me on my long-term sobriety. His medical bedside manner was attentive, and he waited for me to answer. He didn't seem rushed. He was instead accommodating, respectful and polite.

Towards the end of our evaluation, he asked me, "Has anyone ever mentioned bipolar to you?"

I was stunned. I was again faced with a diagnosis I had been running from, a diagnosis I had rejected.

I mentioned that, yes, my psychiatrist back at home had brought up bipolar disorder as a possibility, but that I had not thought much of it since then. The doctor went on to explain that he believed I was, in fact, bipolar. The kind of bipolar disorder I had made me prone to experiencing depressive episodes instead of manic ones.

The doctor continued, "Your previous psychiatrist had been treating you with antidepressants for the past two years. The treatment for bipolar is not with antidepressants, but with bipolar-specific medication."

With that, he prescribed me two different bipolar-specific medications: Lithium and Latuda.

He explained, "Lithium is a medication that restores balance to neurotransmitters in the brain to stabilize extreme emotions and behaviors.[3] In short, it treats bipolar disorder by stabilizing one's mood. It improves mood, sleep, appetite, and energy level. Overall, it can help people think more clearly, feel less nervous, and participate in everyday life. Latuda is a psychiatric medication that works by adjusting levels of certain brain neurotransmitters. A couple of the neurotransmitters it adjusts are dopamine and serotonin."[4]

He mentioned that one of the possible side effects of Latuda is tardive dyskinesia, which is a neurological disorder that causes involuntary movement of the mouth and tongue. The doctor prescribed me these two medications, and, for the first time since I entered either hospital, I felt I was in good hands. I went back to my quarters, had a good cry, and fell into a much-needed sleep.

CHAPTER 6

Denial

A NURSE WOKE ME from my sleep. She informed me I needed to get up, get ready, and join the other patients in the group room.

"Group room? What is that?" I inquired.

She told me it was the room where I would partake in group activities. She then went on to give me the daily itinerary for the duration of my stay:

1. Breakfast at around 6:30 - 7 am.

2. Medication time (when we were given our prescribed meds).

3. Group #1 - Group Therapy.

4. 15 to 20 minute break.

5. Arts and crafts.

6. Lunch at noon.

7. Rest time.

8. Recreation time.

9. Group #2 - Group Education.

10. Lunch at 5 pm.

11. Visitors' hour.

12. Group #3 - Group Reflection.

13. Medication time.

14. Bedtime at 8-9 pm.

WHEN THE NURSE WOKE me up, it was about 10 in the morning, so the first group session of the day had already begun. The nurse escorted me out of my room, through the corridors, to the group room. It was a moderately sized room with chairs set in a circle in the center of it. As I entered, I counted about eight other patients seated, not including the facilitator. I crept in slowly, trying to stay as silent and unnoticeable as possible. I slid into one of the chairs with empty seats on either side.

The facilitator was talking about depression, "Does anyone know the definition of depression? Has anyone ever experienced depression?"

One of the patients responded with a generic response, "It means someone is stuck in a deep sadness."

"Yes, good. That's fairly accurate," The facilitator went on to expand on the definition and to pose the question, "If you've suffered from depression, what are some things you can do to actively combat it? What are some things you have done, or what would you like to do?"

I faded in and out of focus as everyone spoke back and forth. It was a series of small testimonials, shallow half-thought-through answers, and long silent gaps. I hadn't bothered to speak up. I didn't want to be a part of this. I looked down at my hands; my fingers were interlocked across my lap. I focused on spinning my thumbs one around the other. It was captivating, twiddling my thumbs.

❖   ❖   ❖

GROUP WAS FINALLY OVER. I stood up, not knowing what to do or where to go. We had a 15-20 minute break as the staff set up the group room for arts and crafts activities. We were not allowed to return to our rooms, so I spent my break walking slowly to the bathroom and back. It's incredible how slow one must move to eat up a whole 20 minutes. My speed matched that of a snail's.

I returned to the group room and saw the circle of chairs was gone. In their place were two long rectangular tables decorated with art supplies. As I got closer, one of the staff members noticed me. She began to wave her hand at me, ushering me to come sit. I reluctantly took a seat near her, and she went on to tell me about all the different art activities I could do at each station, "We have stacks of magazines down there at the end of the table, you can make collages with those. Next, we have boxes of popsicle sticks you can use to build whatever you'd like. We do a lot of popsicle puppets, but there are so many options! Get creative. Then we have markers...." I began to tune her out as she went on.

I looked up and down the length of the table a few times before I settled on an activity. I took a piece of paper and a marker and placed them in front of me. I stared blankly at the blank sheet of paper for a good while when the same staff member broke me from my trance to ask me what I would make. I looked up at her with no response. I hadn't really thought of anything to draw, I don't think I even had the intention of using the marker and paper. After a pause, I shrugged. She suggested I start by tracing my hand.

I nodded and picked up the marker to make myself look busy. With a satisfied look, she moved on to her next target.

I played with the marker for a while, twisting it around, looking for nothing in particular. After sufficiently twisting it, I pulled the cap off. I was unwilling to think up something to draw for myself, so I did as the staff member suggested. I flattened my left hand with my palm facing down onto the paper and began tracing.

I moved the marker slowly around the curve of my palm. I stopped for a moment to let the ink bleed into the paper, and I watched as the ink soaked in and spread wider and wider. I continued following the form of my hand, tracing it centimeter by centimeter.

All these 'crafts' are so dull... Why do we have to do them anyway?

I eventually finished tracing my hand, but instead of taking it farther and transforming it into something else, I picked up another sheet of paper and began a new drawing.

I tried to do everything slowly. If I can do things slowly, it'll consume more time, and the more time that's eaten up, the less I have to participate in these pointless activities. At least, that was my reasoning.

It was all so lackluster. I had no desire to partake in any of these activities, and I definitely didn't trust anyone else in the facility—not the staff or other patients.

I wonder if they care about me. Perhaps they have no interest in helping me get better.

I was about to finish my third hand portrait when an announcement was made that it was time for lunch. I felt relieved for a moment. At last, I could stop making these useless drawings, but then I remembered that I had to go to the day room for lunch. I was not allowed to join everyone in the dining hall because I was still under the seventy-two-hour observation period.

When I got to the day room, I felt another small sense of relief. There were only three other patients in the day room aside from me. The comfort stemmed from me finding a place I could finally have some space, but on the opposing side, I realized it also meant I could not blend in as well. I would stick out to the staff like a sore thumb here.

The room was made up of a long table with six chairs. It had couches and a TV for lounging, the TV, however, was controlled by staff. It remained off during the day. The day room was also directly across from the nurse's station. That way, they could always keep a watchful eye on us.

I sat quietly and looked down at my lunch, a tuna salad plate. I was losing a staring contest with it. It was of the utmost importance that I win at least one round because I couldn't be bothered to talk to anyone else. I barely touched my food; I mostly nibbled on the side of bread that came with the meal.

Lunch seemed to fly by, and before I knew it, it was rest time. This was the only time during the day we were allowed to return to our rooms. I made my way to my room and went into the bathroom. I stood in front of the thick steel mirror and stared at the figure in front of me. The hospital mirror did not reflect a clear image; instead, it was a warped and distorted image of whatever lay in front of it. I looked at myself, distorted and unrecognizable, with disheveled hair and wrinkled hospital pajamas. I could hardly recognize myself.

I turned away from my reflection. I went to my bed where I slept until rest time was over.

❖   ❖   ❖

ONE OF THE STAFF members woke me. They came to tell me it was time to get up and begin recreation time. Because I was still under the 72-hour observation, I was not allowed to go to the recreation room. I was, however, permitted in the day room. Instead of rushing over there, I let the staff member know I was going to shower and change.

I took my time in the shower. I stood under the running water, feeling the warmth encapsulate me. I let the bathroom fill up with so much steam that it made it challenging to see things clearly. Everything looked hazy.

I knew I couldn't stay in the shower forever, so I begrudgingly shut the water off and stepped out into the room. I walked to my bed where a clean pair of folded hospital pajamas was waiting for me. The hospital ruled that patients *must* change their clothes and shower once daily. These were the minimum requirements.

I changed into my new set of pajamas, and before I knew it, we were off to our second group meeting of the day. I don't know where the time went, I don't even fully remember what it was I was doing, but I did as I was told and began to make my way to the group room.

As I entered the room, I saw it was back to its original setup, with a circle of chairs in the middle. I again pulled myself to the emptiest-looking seat and took a deep breath as I prepared to sit through another long group session.

I would much rather be back in my room, in bed, away from everyone. Actually, I'd very much rather be back at home—my safe haven. No one could bother me there.

The facilitator was looking to the right and left, trying to ensure everyone who was supposed to be there was present and accounted for. Once satisfied, she settled into her chair and began to address us all, "Hi everyone, welcome back to the group. I hope you've all been having a good day. Allow me to introduce you to today's topic. Today, we will be talking and learning about bipolar disorder."

The moment I heard the word "bipolar," my ears perked up, and my stomach dropped. I felt all the heat from my body rush to my head and my hands turned sweaty and clammy. It felt like I had just experienced a steep drop on an extremely tall roller coaster.

Oh no. What have I gotten myself into...

I took a deep gulp to shove down the sudden emotion I was feeling. The facilitator went on, "Does anyone know what bipolar disorder is? How would you define it?"

Silence. No one spoke up. We sat there for what felt like two hours when, in reality, it was probably under a minute.

"Anyone? It's ok if you don't know an exact definition. Anything, just to help us get started. Let's see... who can help us... Mary? How about you, Mary?"

My body immediately tensed at the mention of my name.

No no no no no. Please no.

I looked around. Everyone was looking at me. I crossed my arms and legs, hunched my back, and shrugged my shoulders together to make myself smaller, to disappear.

"Mary? Have any idea of what bipolar disorder is?"

"...I, uh, I don't know." I managed to mumble something, *anything*, out.

Whew.

She moved on to someone else, and I feel my body slightly release some tension. Everyone was reluctant to speak up. It felt like they all knew something, something they were trying to hide from me. They all knew about the discussion I had with my psychiatrist. I know that's impossible, but the air in the room was so thick and heavy that it filled my mind with crazy ideas. I felt fight or flight mode kick in, and I had no choice but to stay and fight.

"Alright, no problem. Allow me to give you a little definition of what bipolar disorder is. Bipolar disorder is a mental illness that can cause sudden and drastic changes in mood. Not only can it affect mood, but it can also affect energy levels and decision-making skills. Those with bipolar can experience extreme highs and lows of emotion, and we refer to these extremes as 'mania.' Has anyone here noticed a sudden shift in emotion? Care to share?"

I looked down at the ground, but it felt like her eyes were on me. I glanced up quickly and saw that she was looking not at me, but around the room at everyone. It didn't matter. I still felt invisible eyes on me, looking right through me. I felt like I was lying to everyone, and they knew.

Someone shared an experience of the time they were having a generally happy day, and then they got some bad news about their job that changed their mood completely. "Excellent! That is a great example. But in this case, there is a clear cause for your sudden shift in emotion; you got bad news. Sometimes, people who are bipolar can switch very quickly without such a cause.

The facilitator went on to define the different types of bipolar disorder, "There are four basic types of bipolar disorder: bipolar I, bipolar II, cyclothymic disorder, and other specified and unspecified bipolar-related disorders."

She got up and began writing on the white board as she spoke:

TYPES OF BIPOLAR ILLNESS

The four basic types of bipolar disorders are:

1. Bipolar I

2. Bipolar II

3. Cyclothymic Disorder

4. Other

"I'M GOING TO GO through each one with you today. Let's start with bipolar I disorder. Bipolar I has a couple of indicators: it can be identified by manic episodes that last at least seven days or by manic episodes that are so severe the person needs immediate hospital care. Usually, depressive episodes occur as well, typically lasting at least two weeks. It's also possible that those with Bipolar I experience episodes of depression with mixed features. For example, it's possible for them to

have depression and manic symptoms simultaneously." She wrote this on the board under the "Bipolar I"
section. She continued to write the definition she was
giving to the corresponding type.

"Next, we have bipolar II disorder. Bipolar II can
be recognized through a pattern of depressive and
hypomanic episodes, but not the full-blown manic
episodes we might see in bipolar I."

*Bipolar II... it's defined by a pattern of depres-
sive episodes and hypomanic episodes, but not full-
blown manic episodes. I must have bipolar II.*

"Then we have cyclothymic disorder. This disorder is defined by numerous periods of hypomanic
symptoms and depressive symptoms, which last for
at least two years. The symptoms do not meet the di-
agnostic requirements for a hypomanic episode and
a depressive episode."

"Last, but not least (because it encapsulates many more), we have other specified and unspecified Bipolar and related disorders. These are made up of bipolar disorder symptoms that do not match the three categories listed above."[5]

She began to write a separate section on the board. It read: **SIGNS AND SYMPTOMS**. When she finished writing, she turned back to the group and began speaking about the signs and symptoms, "The signs and symptoms for people with bipolar disorder are periods of unusually intense emotion. This can include changes in sleep patterns, activity levels, and unusual behaviors. These distinct periods are called 'mood episodes' and drastically differ from the moods and behaviors typical for the person."

She wrote out on the board:

SYMPTOMS OF MANIC EPISODES

- Feeling very up, high, or elated

- Increased energy

- Increased activity levels

- Feeling jumpy or wired

- Trouble sleeping

- Talking fast about a lot of different things

- Being agitated, irritable, or touchy

- Doing risky things

SYMPTOMS OF DEPRESSIVE EPISODES

- Feeling very sad, down, empty, or hopeless

- Decreased energy

- Decreased activity levels

- Trouble sleeping, sleeping too much or too little

- Feeling like they can't enjoy anything

- Feeling worried and empty

- Trouble concentrating

- Forgetfulness

- Eating too much or too little
- Feeling tired[6]

AFTER EXHAUSTING THE LISTS of symptoms of both manic and depressive episodes, she continued her talk, "There is no single cause of bipolar disorder. Instead, it's most likely that many factors contribute to the illness. Some research has suggested that people with certain genes are more likely to develop bipolar disorder than others. That said, genes are not the only risk factor for bipolar disorder. Studies have been done where a set of identical twins are looked at to see if they develop the same disorder. The results show that if one twin develops bipolar disorder, the other twin does not always develop the disorder. This is despite the fact that identical twins share the same genes."

"Now that we are on the topic of genetics, bipolar disorder tends to run in families. Children with a parent or sibling with bipolar disorder are more likely to develop the illness compared with children who don't have a family history of the disorder."[7]

"Thankfully, treatments and therapies are in place to help people—even those with the most severe form of bipolar disorder—to better control their symptoms. An effective treatment plan usually includes a combination of medication and psychotherapy. Bipolar disorder is a lifelong illness that may need continuous treatment. Episodes of mania and depression typically come back over time. Between episodes, many people are free of mood changes. Some medications for bipolar disorder include mood stabilizers, atypical antipsychotics, and antidepressants."[8]

She continued, talking about the upsides to a lifetime disorder. She had an encouraging tone, but it became background noise as she continued talking.

❖   ❖   ❖

IT WAS FINALLY DINNER time, and I couldn't be more relieved to leave the group room. I'm unsure how I made it through the group meeting, but I did. I was a bit shaky by the end. I felt winded, as if I had just gone for a brisk run.

For dinner, I went back to the day room. We were served pasta with meatballs, a side salad, and jello for dessert. Oh, and of course milk. We were given milk with every meal.

I didn't want dinner to end because I knew that after dinner came visitor's hour. I was stuck in Santa Rosa, over two hours away from my friends or family. I tried my best not to think about it.

I looked down at my plate of spaghetti. I twirled one noodle around my fork, lifted it to my mouth, and ate it. I then pushed around the meatballs for a while. Perhaps if I ate slowly, time would follow suit. That way, dinner wouldn't end, and I wouldn't have to be alone during visitor's hour.

Despite my best efforts, dinner did pass. It was suddenly visiting hour. I couldn't help holding back the surge of sadness any longer. I felt tears well up in my eyes and spill out onto my cheeks. I tried to wipe them quickly so no one would notice, but it was no use. They kept coming.

People were heading off to the visitor's room while I stayed back in the day room. I tried to stop the tears from coming, but at this point, I felt that my eyes were puffy from crying.

A nurse noticed me after a few minutes and approached me, asking why I was sad. I told her none of my family was here, so I had no one to visit. I was all alone.

"Is there any way I can call my daughter? I haven't spoken with her since I was at the last hospital."

The nurse agreed to let me call my daughter, and I felt a massive wave of relief from the sadness I was feeling. The nurse took me to the nurse's station and handed me a landline phone. I dialed my daughter's number and waited for her to pick up.

"Hello?"

"Hi, honey, it's mom."

"Mom? Oh my goodness, where are you? I've been trying to reach you for two days. God! I called the ER but they refused to tell me where you were. I called every local hospital to find you—where are you?? I called your psychiatrist and he wouldn't tell me because of some kind of confidentiality act. I even called your sister Marie and your brother Kevin."

"Oh honey, I'm so sorry. I'm at a locked facility in Santa Rosa. I got so depressed, and it kept getting worse. I'm in a safe place."

"Oh my God! That's so far away."

"I know. They moved me in the middle of the night and said it was the only bed available."

"How long will you be there?"

"I don't know."

"Mom, I'm so relieved you called and you're ok. Can you call me again and let me know when you'll be discharged?"

"Ok, honey, I love you."

"I love you too."

I hung up the phone and looked at the clock. It was 7:19 pm. I called my daughter the day I admitted myself to the ER to let her know where I was, but after that, I had no way to contact her. She was left wondering where I was and if I was ok for over a day and a half. I felt guilty that I had left her in the dark, worried and stressed. But I didn't have a choice, without my phone, I couldn't have called her sooner even if I wanted to, and believe me, I did want to.

It was so comforting to hear my daughter's voice. At the same time, knowing what a burden I'd become was hard.

At 7:30, visitor's hour ended, and group reflection began. I hardly listened. Instead, I spent the time thinking about my daughter and my grandsons back home.

Group reflection went by in a flash, and by the time I knew it, I was medicated and tucked away in bed. I was still thinking about my daughter. My thoughts spread to my friends and the community I had always been a part of.

I felt a deep emptiness inside my chest as I drifted to sleep. It weighed me down. Over 100 miles away from home in a room shared with a stranger, stuck in a hospital full of even more strangers, I felt lonelier than I'd ever been.

CHAPTER 7

Trying to Accept My Reality

WHEN I WAS FIRST admitted, I only had the pajamas from the ER. My personal clothes were transported here in the same ambulance, but I was not permitted to have them. In my anxiety-ridden state, I hadn't packed anything for a long stay, so the hospital lent me some clothes from the "left behind locker" (clothes from former patients). The clothes were too big and mismatched, but they were clean and better than the hospital pajamas. I did the best I could with what I was given. I chose a large oversized gray t-shirt and brown baggy sweatpants. When I returned to my quarters from my trip to the left-behind locker, I changed in the bathroom. I looked in the 'mirror' on the wall and saw a distorted image of a homeless-looking woman. It didn't look like me.

Not only did I not have my own clothes, but I was also without my toiletries. I didn't have any face cleanser, moisturizer, or makeup. I just did without. Upon admitting myself, I had been so sick and depressed that I couldn't think through the process of what was about to happen: that I would be admitted, potentially for days on end. I couldn't think of anything to pack, not clothes, toiletries, or anything else I may have needed. Not having these things was incredibly embarrassing; my disheveled and undone physical appearance only added to my negative self-image. I lacked any confidence that I was worthy.

For the next couple of days, I continued to seclude myself. Along with the group meetings, I had daily one-on-one sessions with my psychiatrist who continuously gave me words of encouragement. I still had a fog hindering me... The majority of my first few days felt like faint, fading memories. As the days went by, I slowly began to feel safe, but I also felt medicated at the same time. After the third day, I felt my medication begin to work. I noticed this when I was no longer hindered by incessant suicidal thoughts. I was, however, still extremely depressed.

Once I noticed the change in my thinking, I realized that I would never get out of this place, this situation, if I didn't make some changes. I knew if I continued to keep to myself, if I went on without participating, I would get nowhere.

After 72 hours, I was released from the 5150 hold and, per my psychiatrist's suggestion, placed on a 5250. A 5250 extends one's stay for up to two weeks. He explained my right to fight this decision. I was aware I wasn't yet myself and found no reason to oppose this treatment plan. His professional opinion was that I should stay and continue treatment, and I trusted his decision. On the 5250, I would continue attending daily evaluations with the psychiatrist, continue to be monitored by staff, and continue attending all the group therapy and informational mental health sessions. This new hold meant I was allowed to line up with the other patients for meals, meds, groups, and recreation.

I was previously a nurse consultant in the California Department of Corrections and Rehabilitation. This experience led me to witness inmates having to line up for everything, meals, meds, recreational activities, jobs, etc. I couldn't help but wonder if this was how prisoners felt.

As a registered nurse, I knew the expectations and why staff observed me. Unlike a medical hospital where your vital signs, level of consciousness, lab tests, etc., are closely monitored, in a psychiatric facility, all the patient's behaviors are observed. Included in their observations are:

- *Appearance*: well-dressed and well-groomed or poorly groomed and dirty, ability to do self-care or poor hygiene

- *Behavior motor activity*: agitation, pacing, restless mood, depressed, euphoric, elated, anxious or angry, speech pressures—loud or soft

- *Thought processes*: illogical, delusional, coherent, and goal-oriented

- *Thought content*: suicidal, worthlessness, hopelessness, grandiose or bizarre

- *Perception*: illusions or hallucinations

- *Sensorium*: clear or sedated

- *Insight*: good or poor

- *Judgment*: good or poor

- *Compliance*: resistant or cooperative

- *Cognitive concentration*: short attention span, confusion, memory short-term mild impairment confusion, long-term memory intact, mild impairment to marked impairment

EVERY FIFTEEN MINUTES, A staff member checked on each patient. They constantly observed and documented:

- Individual sleep patterns
- How much was eaten at each meal
- Ability and desire to do self-care
- AWOL risk
- Group attendance and participation
- Suicidal or self-harm thoughts
- Relationship interaction both with staff and other residents
- Medication compliance
- Any other medical issues

I HAD HIGH BLOOD pressure instability which required periodic blood pressure readings and adjusting my blood pressure medication. All this happened on a 24-hour basis, seven days a week. Even though I was still depressed, I hit all the right marks in all the right areas in the observation category.

My knowledge of this system wasn't to be better than anyone else or to impress the staff. I utilized my knowledge to regain a sliver of control in my uncontrollable life. Not for power or sway, but to help myself get better and be an active part of the 'fix me team.' It's not knowledge that gives control, but the use of that knowledge for your benefit. God knew I wanted to get better, and God knew I deserved to get better. Thanks to Him, I had a nursing background to prepare me for this moment.

CHAPTER 8

Breaking Through

FROM THAT POINT ON, after my first three days of self-imposed alienation, I made the conscious decision to actively participate in my treatment plan to the best of my ability. I was slowly feeling better, I no longer felt suicidal, and I attributed this to my medication starting to kick in.

Quite a few changes were happening with my stay. I was now allowed to go to the patient's dining room and have meals with the rest of the patients. The dining room was a nice change of scenery—actual windows filled the room with natural light. There were about 20 other patients in total, and I made it a goal to sit with a different group of people every meal.

I also tried to speak up and contribute to the discussion during each group session at least once or twice. It could be challenging at times since some of the subject matter was so serious and deep, but I pushed myself to speak up when it felt uncomfortable.

Uncomfortable or not, I knew that showing effort would have an internal effect on me, even if that effect was a slow one. It would also serve to show the nurses and the rest of the staff that I was making an effort. Slowly, the effects of this involvement began to emerge. I was feeling less alone and more 'a part of.'

❖   ❖   ❖

IT WAS LOVELY TO have access to the main dining area. Having natural light fill a space brought me comfort, and there was a beautiful view of blossoming flowers and green trees outside the window that made me feel serene. During my first meal in the cafeteria, I approached a table with two other ladies and introduced myself, "Hi, my name is Mary. This is my first time in the cafeteria."

I was greeted with two polite, reserved smiles.

"Hi. My name's Charlotte," one woman responded.

Charlotte looked to be in her 30s. She wore a matching dark blue sweat suit with a white turtleneck underneath.

"And this is Patricia," she introduced me to the other lady. Patricia looked to be in her 60s. She wore dark blue denim jeans and a red turtleneck sweater.

They were open to me joining them, so I took a seat, and we began to chat. Our conversation centered around why we were here. We didn't really touch on what we did for a living, and I made sure not to mention that I was a nurse. I do this in most settings because people tend to bombard me with their medical issues. I was here as a patient, not a nurse.

It was all very vague when it came to subject matters such as these. My answer to what I did was that I'm retired. No further explanation was needed. There was no family talk, no talk about where we lived, where we grew up, or what our hobbies were. It was entirely centered around where we were and what we were struggling with internally.

Keeping the conversation at this level felt safe. I was still very distrustful. I didn't *want* to share intimate details of my life with others, but in this setting, it was the safest subject matter to discuss with other patients.

I shared that this was my fourth day here, that I had been struggling with depression, and that I was now struggling with my new diagnosis of bipolar disorder.

Although Charlotte had been the first to initiate introductions, she got quiet, and Patricia spoke up more. Patricia suffered from severe depression as well. She had been there for a week and was preparing to be discharged. She was quite nervous about it.

It was interesting to share such intimate information with people you've just met. We were all here for one reason or another, all under the umbrella of mental health struggles, so that was the best and most comfortable way to relate with one another.

Mealtime was only a half hour, and because the time was so short, it was challenging to maintain a conversation while eating. Our meal was coming to an end, so it was time to finish what we could and then bus our trays. We were not allowed to leave the cafeteria with any food, so a staff member would check to see how much we'd eaten and that we hadn't held onto any snacks for later.

The three of us lined up, dropped off our plates, were checked for food, and then went our separate ways.

❖　　❖　　❖

WHEN IT CAME TIME for recreational activities, we were all escorted to the recreational room. The recreational room was another reward I received upon exiting my 72-hour observation hold. This room had a variety of activities available for us: hoops and a court for basketball, a large track for walking, bean bags for tossing, ping-pong tables, and a table for wiffle ball.

I chose to walk around the perimeter of the basketball court on the track. A couple of other patients were also walking around the perimeter. One of them approached me and said, "I haven't seen you here before."

"Oh, yeah, I'm new. I've been here for four days. Today was my first day out of the 72-hour hold."

He was a gentleman in his 50s. He walked beside me at my pace and asked, "So, how's it going?"

"It's going, that's for sure. Today I'm surprisingly feeling pretty hopeful about things."

He was a very pleasant man. He didn't tell me why he was here, only that he had been on a 72-hour hold as well.

After we exchanged pleasantries, he took off and walked at a much faster pace. I watched as he revealed his true speed, and his figure grew smaller the farther he went.

After walking around several times, I went over to sit on some benchers. A couple of minutes later, I noticed a woman holding a ball, looking at me. It looked as though she was trying to get my attention. She held the ball up in the air and gave me a warning wave, then she bent her arm back, rounded it over her shoulder, and released the ball. It flew through the air at me and I caught it with no problem, thanks to her heads up.

She walked over to me and yelled, "Let's play catch!" She introduced herself, "My name is Arlene. I'm the activities director. I haven't seen you around here. You're new, right?"

"Yes, I am."

"Awesome! I think it will add to your day to have meals and recreation time with the rest of our group."

We played a friendly game of catch for the remainder of recreation time. We were prompted to return to the unit for our end-of-the-day group reflection. On my way over to group discussion, I couldn't help but compare the friendliness of Arlene to the stoic and impartial attitude of the nursing staff.

During the group reflection discussion, I truly took the time to think back on my day and how things went. I reflected on how nice it felt to be in the cafeteria with all the other patients, and how welcoming it was because of the windows that allowed natural lighting and a green view. I thought about my general interactions with the other patients; they had all been so pleasant and friendly. It was also a good experience to be active in the recreation room.

When it came my turn to talk about how my day went, I shared all this and more with everyone. I found that openly discussing my depression and experiences with others made me feel less alone.

What surprised me, though, was how intently I found myself listening to everyone else instead of talking or asking questions. Hearing their stories and sharing mine—I began to feel more human.

I left that session more determined to be an active player in my treatment. I felt a glimmer of hope form within me, hope that I had the potential to get better.

CHAPTER 9

Goodbye and Good Luck

SIX DAYS INTO MY stay, I'd kept up with my goal of being more involved, but I wasn't seeing quite the progression I hoped. My depression was somewhat lifted, but I still wasn't myself. The biggest improvement so far was that I no longer felt suicidal. Not being suicidal was a welcomed change, but I was still emotionally fragile. My emotions felt delicate, like a vase teetering on the edge of a cliff. Sometimes I felt safer, farther away from the cliff. Other times, like I was peering down into the blackness below. And during some unwarranted moments, it felt like I was falling.

It was after breakfast but before our first group meeting, and I went to have my one-on-one meeting with the psychiatrist. I had no expectations for this meeting, all our daily meetings so far had been beneficial. He had always been encouraging and attentive.

I entered the office. There was a different air about the room. I greeted the psychiatrist, and he greeted me back. His tone was different as well, it had shifted. Our past meetings had been more open and relaxed. I would come in and sit for a moment while he finished up whatever he was doing on his computer. Once finished, he would sit there with his hands resting on the arms of his chair, body angled towards me, listening to what I had to share. This time, he was not occupied with his computer. He was waiting for me, with his hands resting on his desk, fingers interlocked. He meant business.

GOODBYE AND GOOD LUCK

"You are to be discharged tomorrow."

I felt my jaw fall open and my mouth form an 'O.' I was shocked. There's no way I'm ready. I wasn't in a suitable state for this decision.

"I—I'm not ready."

"Yes, you are, Mary. We have you on a high dose of Lithium, you've improved, you are no longer suicidal, and that's the criteria for discharge."

I felt panic. I wasn't a part of the decision-making. No one had consulted with me. It was an announcement, not a question.

Nonetheless on June 25th, 2018 six days after admission, I was discharged home with orders to follow up with my primary psychiatrist. I was discharged on Lithium and Latuda. Though not suicidal, I was still very depressed. I still felt so afraid. I knew my depression was looming, but I was on my way home.

We spent the rest of the meeting reviewing how my discharge would go. Different from other medical treatments in the past, the follow-up for this psychiatric stay was entirely my responsibility. I remember when I had my hip and knee replaced, it was medically ordered that I go to a step-down rehabilitation center for intensive physical therapy. Homecare followed that with a visiting nurse and therapist services to enhance and facilitate my post-hospital rehabilitation.

No follow-up was scheduled after my discharge. There was no consultation with my long-term personal psychiatrist, no set follow-up appointment, no home evaluation visit to see how I was progressing on the new medication, and no assessment of my home environment or my support system. I was completely on my own. I even had to find my own transportation for the 100-mile ride back to my house.

I was not included in the decision-making of my discharge. There was no patient conference to discuss my aftercare plan. Instead, I was handed a piece of paper that told me to contact a personal psychiatrist at home, and that's it. They gave me a prescription for a 30-day supply of medication that must be picked up at a pharmacy and nothing more. It felt like I was being pushed out the door with little to no help.

Once discharged, I was going to need a ride home, some 100-plus miles away. I didn't have my car with me, it was still sitting back in the parking lot of the previous hospital. There was no way I was going to pay for a two-hour uber, so I had to call my daughter. There was no one else that would come out all this way to pick me up.

Once I left my meeting with the psychiatrist, I went to the nurse's station to call my daughter. It was a difficult call to make. I knew she would be upset with me.

After a few rings, she picked up.

"Hi honey, it's Mom. The doctor just told me I'll be discharged tomorrow morning. I don't have my car with me, and the hospital doesn't offer a ride back. Can you come and pick me up?"

"Oh God, Mom, that's gonna be difficult. The boys need to be dropped off and picked up for school and I have yard duty at the school. Goodness gracious... How is this gonna work? Is there anyone else who can pick you up?"

"No, honey, I'm afraid not."

"It'll have to be later in the day, after I pick up the kids, sometime between four and five. Depending on traffic, oh my God, that means rush hour traffic both ways. Oh, Jesus."

"I'm sorry, honey."

"Well, there's no other way. I guess I'll see you when I get there."

"Bye honey, I love you."

"Bye."

After our call, I returned to the groups and continued all the mandated activities. Each passing hour filled me with more anticipatory anxiety. The group meetings felt useless. I didn't have time to prepare myself mentally for this discharge decision. There was a void feeling in everything I did, I felt dissociated from my body which made it hard to think and even to speak. This didn't feel real.

❖   ❖   ❖

IT WAS HARD TO sleep, I couldn't shake this feeling of unsteadiness. I was not prepared to leave. I felt like an uncooked batch of chocolate chip cookies being taken out of the oven too soon. I was bound to fall apart.

I felt very similar to how I felt yesterday, only more tired today due to lack of sleep. My anxiety continued to grow.

Who would've thought that I would be against leaving this place? My initial desire when I was first brought here was to run back to the comfort of my home. But I knew that wasn't the right thing to do, I knew that running away would only prolong and progress my mental health crisis. So I stayed. And now, now I'm being forced to leave when I still don't feel ready.

Dudum dudum dudum. I felt my heart pound in my chest.

My daughter wouldn't arrive until later in the afternoon, so I had to go on with the daily itinerary. I felt my heart beat harder and faster as my pickup time ventured nearer.

❖   ❖   ❖

WHEN MY DAUGHTER ARRIVED to pick me up, she had to call the front desk to inform them of her arrival. I was

only given back my belongings after they got confir-
mation that she was here waiting for me.

The clothes I got back were dirty and stained, so
I left the hospital with patient locker clothes. I got my
purse and phone back as well, but I didn't check the
phone, nor did I look in my purse. I was still in shock
that I was being discharged.

I was escorted to the lobby where my daughter
and two grandsons were waiting for me. I felt myself
shrink when I saw my daughter for the first time in
weeks. I was so afraid of how upset she might be, all
I wanted to do was rectify this situation.

We greeted each other with hellos, mine being
timid, hers being curt. I struggled to maintain direct
eye contact with her. Her gaze felt fiery, and I knew
I was to blame. I was given discharge papers and another synopsis of what I should do after discharge,
and then we were on our way.

It was a long and quiet ride. My daughter sat upright in the driver's seat, both arms outstretched with each hand gripping the wheel. Her eyes were fixed on the road ahead of us. I sat next to her in the passenger's seat, idly looking out the window at the trees, or the buildings, or whatever else was outside the window at the time.

During periods like these, there was a role reversal between mother and daughter that made it difficult for her. I was very anxious and aware of her anger. I had a noticeable emptiness inside, and part of that emptiness was falling short as a mother. Once again, I was filled with shame about another crisis that was brought on by me.

My two grandchildren played with each other in the back seat. I mentally thanked God that they were in the car so I could talk with them. It was a long ride back to our hometown, and I was ridden with guilt and dread the whole way. All I could do was try to distract myself by chatting with my grandchildren or immersing myself in the landscape outside.

CHAPTER 10

OH GOD, Where Are You

My daughter dropped me off at the hospital where I parked my car the week before. It had only been one week since I left this parking lot. As my daughter drove off, I pressed a kiss into the palm of my hand and blew it to my grandsons. With a smile on their faces, they blew a kiss back.

From the parking lot, I drove home all alone. I had another long drive ahead of me. It would be another 45-minute drive on the freeway before I reached home. I stayed in the slowest lane for the duration of the ride as I was somewhat shaky. The high dosage of Lithium I was on made me weak, shaky, and drowsy. As I got closer to home, I was relieved to see familiar streets and landmarks. Despite being in my hometown, I felt the loss of a big part of myself. My body felt lighter, like a house of cards, yet my mind felt heavier, like a heavy cloud full of thunder. I had never experienced this feeling before.

I was so far away from my old life. Would I ever be able to get back? It was as if a piece of my soul was gone, left behind somewhere along the way. Would I ever return to normal? Would I be prepared to face life's challenges again?

A mile from my house, I stopped at the pharmacy to get my new prescriptions. I was too ashamed to park and go inside. I was still wearing the second-hand clothes the hospital had given me, and I was petrified of the possibility that someone I knew might be there to see me in all my lowliness. I instead used the drive-up window. The pharmacist at the window gave me the 30-day supply of my new medications and told me I needed to contact my psychiatrist for refills before I ran out.

"Great, thanks." I drove off with the white bag full of my new medications sitting in the passenger's seat next to me.

Once I reached my house, the first thing I did was call my primary psychiatrist. I was given an appointment right away. Once I hung up the phone, I realized I had no discharge summary from my hospital stay to provide him. I was surprised to learn that the current "standard of care" in psychiatry is that when a person is put in a psychiatric hospital, the inpatient psychiatrist doesn't consult with the patient's primary medical doctor or psychiatrist who treats the patient day-to-day. So when it came time for the appointment, I just told my primary psychiatrist what I could remember.

I showed him my 30-day supply of Lithium and Latuda. After his clinical assessment, he added Lamictal to my medication regime. Lamictal is an anticonvulsant used to treat seizures and bipolar disorder by preventing extreme mood swings.

One of the side effects of my new medication was an increase in confusion, and before long, it was apparent I would not be driving myself anywhere anytime soon. My means of transportation to and from my psychiatrist's office turned into a Lyft ride. For those that may be unfamiliar with what Lyft is, it's a transportation service that has drivers pick you up from your location and take you to your set destination. It's pretty much a taxi service, except much less expensive. The more than 60-mile round-trip Lyft cost me about $65.

Despite losing my driving ability, I tried my best to resume daily activities, such as swimming, lunches, and AA meetings. My friends were kind enough to chauffeur me to all these activities. But most days, I failed to attend.

In July, my AA and Alanon Group hosted an annual spiritual women's retreat that I've participated in for the past 15 years. This retreat had always been a replenishing weekend for me, so I was looking forward to a period of restoration, especially in light of all my mental struggles. The retreat was held at a Catholic retreat center and lasted one weekend. The theme of this year's retreat was all about self-forgiveness.

The center was a stunning location. It was a tranquil, serene property. The building we were staying in was quiet. From the outside, it looked like a two-story dormitory. Once entered, the interior had dim lighting and big windows in every room. It was a large and empty space everywhere you went. It felt like walking through the hallways at a Hogwarts study hall.

There were about 40 women on this retreat, and each got their own room. Every room had a bed, a desk, and a sitting chair because in between meetings they wanted you to go back to your room and contemplate everything that was discussed. Aside from the 40 women spending the whole weekend at the convent, there were also 20 'day-trippers' who would come just for the day. We had a meeting room where we were expected to gather daily. This room was a former library for the nuns, so it had tall walls with built-in bookshelves filled with religious texts.

Outside the building was a circular garden with many winding paths going in, around, and through it. The repetitive circular paths that made up the garden seemed to encourage meditation for those walking in it. This garden also separated our building from the chapel that the nuns attended. The chapel room for the nuns was separate from the area we were allotted for our retreat. The chapel we had for the retreat was inside the same building. It was a large room—just large enough to seat around 50 people. It had an entire wall of glass behind the altar, and just beyond the glass was a large oak tree towering over us all. The venue we stayed at had all the components necessary to foster spiritual healing.

I was looking forward to this weekend being some magic fix to the uneasiness I had felt since I left the hospital. Heck, ever since I even *went* to the hospital. Seeing the beautiful decor and serene landscape made me hopeful that this weekend was just what I needed.

I knew most women on this trip with me. I'd gone to meetings with them for years and have always been deeply invested in my AA community. However, as I greeted everyone and maintained pleasantries, I found it difficult to connect with any of my longtime friends. I was still extremely spiritually, physically, and emotionally bankrupt. Deep down, I hoped being with them in this place would fill me back up. But this bankruptcy prevented me from soaking up all their support. It made it difficult to accept their love.

My friends clearly noticed the decline in my mental state. I was conversationally off; whenever I tried to insert myself into any dialogue, my participation steadily tapered off. I felt uncontrollable—as if I would burst into tears at any unsuspecting moment. And sometimes I did. Because of these overwhelming fits, I quickly found my attention pulled from talking and fixed on finding the nearest exit.

All the women offered me comfort, but their efforts were no use. I couldn't let anyone in. Although I had known these women for years and considered them all my friends, there was still this part of me that was unable to trust them. I prayed that God would restore my sanity. I still couldn't bring forth the part of me that had made good accomplishments, good achievements, or good connections in my life.

❖   ❖   ❖

THE WEEKEND AWAY DID not provide the spiritual re-
plenishment I needed. I was back home from the retreat and out of the hospital for less than five weeks.
Despite my best efforts, there was no question that
my depression was back.

I was labile, sad, and lost interest in day-to-day
matters. I had two car accidents caused directly by
my mental confusion. No one was with me, but in
the second accident, my car was totaled. After having
gone five weeks without driving since my discharge
from the hospital, my anxiety levels had peaked, and
through all my confusion and stress, I permitted myself to drive.

With my increased mental confusion, I shouldn't
have been driving. In hindsight, I was in denial about
how bad I was feeling. I was also terrified of another breakdown, another nightmare, another piece of
my soul lost, and another hospitalization. I was so

scared that I had tried to reinstate a level of normalcy I could not attain.

Despite doing all the recommended medical treatment, my summer was filled with increased depression and anxiety. I feared I would be like this for the rest of my life.

In an act of desperation, I got on a waiting list for electroconvulsive therapy (ECT). On Tuesday, August 21, 2018, I checked into a psychiatric center for electroconvulsive therapy. I was so desperate, so miserable, and so hopeless. It felt like I had tried *everything* to get better, and nothing was working. Here I was, post-hospitalization, on new medication, doing whatever I could to be sane, yet I was still depressed. What was going wrong? Why was it all not working? I was doing everything I could.

From my experience as a nurse, I understood that ECT is an electric shock sent to the brain to trigger a seizure with the hope that it would somehow reduce the effect of depression. However, after looking into it further, there have been multiple theories on how ETCs work. These theories involve the impact of ECT on brain circuitry, activating inactive circuits, and dampening circuits that are overactive. A substantial negative effect of ECT is memory loss.

I only did five ECT treatments. I was too anxious to continue and had no confidence in the doctor. The treatment took place in the doctor's office beside his desk. Every time I went into his office, it felt like I was entering a storage closet. It was a small, cramped room with no windows. Stacked furniture was pushed all against the back and side walls. The doctor's desk was an old-fashioned oak roll-top desk cluttered with papers covering every square inch of its surface.

A nurse would roll the stretcher right next to his desk to perform the procedure. Once I was laying on the stretcher, an anesthesiologist would come in and put me under. I would wake up in the recovery room, not knowing what had happened. I never knew how long the procedure took or how long I was in the recovery room. The experience felt very unprofessional, and I didn't feel safe in the slightest.

❖   ❖   ❖

By September 1, 2018, ten weeks after discharge from the psychiatric hospital, my depression had worsened significantly. I was now suffering from short-term memory loss as a result of the ECT, I wasn't caring for my daily bathing and grooming, I had difficulty remembering people's names as well as the names of my medications, I got lost going to familiar places, I no longer had an appetite, my hands had tremors, and I had such difficulty walking that I needed assistance.

A nurse friend called and mentioned that she visited me during one of my ECT treatments to offer comfort and reassurance.

"Hi Mary, it's Alex. How have you been?"

"Oh hi, Alex. I've been ok. How are you?"

"I'm fine, I'm fine. I'm just calling to check and see how you've been holding up after your last, uh, treatment. It's a relief to hear your voice. I was really, really worried about you."

"My last treatment? Oh, you mean my ECT treatment?"

"Yeah."

"How did you know I just had a treatment done?"

"Mary, I was with you."

"You were?"

"Yes!"

"Oh dear, I don't remember you being there... To be honest, I don't ever remember much of what happens after the treatments."

"Well, do you remember me driving you home? Or the magazines I left for you to look at on your coffee table?"

"No..." I looked over at my coffee table and saw a small stack of magazines laying on it. I had no recollection of her visit *at all.*

We finished up the phone call with her telling me to take care of myself and me agreeing to try.

A few nights later, another friend of mine took me out for dinner before my weekly AA meeting. She picked me up at my house. When I got into the car, she gave me a confused smile. There was a bit of shock behind her eyes.

"Hey! Oh—Are you doing alright, Mary?"

"Hi, Sue. Yes, why do you ask?"

"Oh—it's just, you're not usually so... unkempt."

I just turned my head and stared out the window as we drove to Panera. When we pulled into the parking lot, Sue said, "Listen, Mary, you don't seem all that prepared to go out in public and eat or go to your meeting. I know you. You're usually very concerned with your appearance. It's not that you're not still beautiful and all, but I think it's best if we take the food to go. What do you say?"

She was right. I looked down at myself. I wore the same clothes I had put on at the beginning of the week—a stained blue t-shirt and pajama pants. I hadn't showered since the last time I changed my clothes. In the best possible manner, my friend was politely advising me that I would not want to be seen out in public with such poor hygiene. I agreed to her suggestion and we ordered our food to go.

The next day, Sue and another friend, Penny, offered to drive me to an upcoming doctor's appointment. When the day of the appointment came, I took my two friends to the wrong facility in the entirely wrong city. After confusedly wandering around, my friends saw that I was unable to walk straight. They went into the medical facility and got me a wheelchair. I was so confused then that I don't remember any of this. They told me in the aftermath just how bad my health had declined.

They directed me back to the car and used my phone to call my primary doctor. When someone picked up the phone, it was the department operator. They told the operator to connect them to the doctor and that it was an emergency. With no further pushback, they were directed to the doctor's line. Once filled in, she told them to take me to the nearest hospital ER immediately. I will always be grateful to them for getting me the help I needed.

CHAPTER 11

OH GOD — Not Again!

ON OCTOBER 5, 2018, 13 weeks after discharge from the psychiatric hospital, I was admitted to the acute care hospital for lithium toxicity, thyroid toxicity, poor nutrition, dehydration, acute renal failure, acute kidney injury, and acute metabolic encephalopathy.

The doctor told me my confusion may have caused me to make mistakes in my daily lithium dosing. I had most likely unintentionally increased my daily dosage, subjecting me to much stronger side effects.

In the acute care hospital, I was still very confused and frightened. I hadn't been eating or drinking much for the past few weeks, so I was fragile and dehydrated. I was so weak that I was unable to walk alone safely. To rehydrate my body, I was given IV fluids and was hooked up to a monitor that read my heart rate, blood pressure, and pulse. I was essentially bound to my bed. I needed physical therapy twice daily to learn how to transfer from a bed to a wheelchair.

Due to the lithium toxicity diagnosis, the lithium was discontinued immediately, and a psychiatric consult was ordered to review my medications. The care plan was to continue with the Lamictal and Latuda as previously prescribed.

I stayed at the acute care hospital for four days. Before my discharge, we held a patient care conference to discuss the next steps. I couldn't care for myself at home alone—I was dependent on others for all my daily living activities. I couldn't shower or dress, I couldn't grocery shop or cook, I couldn't *walk*. My gait was very unsteady, which made me reliant on a wheelchair for transportation. I had never been so weak.

My daughter was present at this conference. During the discussion, she agreed she would not be available to help care for me. Her time was fully committed to her three sons, a husband, and a part time job. The only feasible plan of action for me was to go to a rehabilitation center until I could regain my strength.

On October 8, 2018, I was discharged from the acute care hospital and transferred by ambulance to a skilled nursing facility for rehabilitation. The drive to the nursing facility was much shorter than the drive to Santa Rosa. It was a mere 20-minute ride. When the ambulance arrived, the driver assisted me off the stretcher into a wheelchair. He wheeled me to the lobby where a nurse's aide met us. She greeted me with a warm smile and wheeled me off to the room I'd be staying in.

On the way there, I made mental observations on positive things I noticed. One of my nursing jobs in the past was to do annual on-site visits to relicense and certify skilled nursing facilities. The team I was a part of looked at a number of aspects in the facilities we certified: medication passes, meal preparation and delivery, facility cleanliness, staffing ratio, and timeliness in responding to patient call lights. These were only a few of the observations made by team members.

The facility was older, but it was clean and had no odors. Over the next few weeks, it met all the standards I was familiar with monitoring. In fact, the staffing ratio exceeded the requirement and had more RNs per shift than mandated by law.

When we got to my room, however, I was sorely disappointed. The room was dark and gloomy with drawn shades. It was overcrowded with three beds, plus miscellaneous equipment like wheelchairs, walkers, chairs, and bedside tables. We also had to share a bathroom with three other patients in the next bedroom.

The nurse's aide took all my vital signs in the room. Once we were done, she informed me that the nurse would be in shortly. About 15 minutes went by, and during that time I got to know just how cramped the space felt. I felt like a mouse going through a maze. There was no room to navigate my wheelchair, and I wasn't yet strong enough to pull myself out of positions I would get stuck in. Within those 15 minutes of waiting, I realized that the only way to maintain any semblance of sanity would be to get out of the room as much as possible.

❖   ❖   ❖

FINALLY, THE NURSE CAME in. She reviewed the doctor's orders and gave me a rundown of what I could expect in the coming weeks.

She told me, "Your daily routine is going to be busy. You will wake up at 5 am for medication. This will be followed by breakfast in bed at 7 am. As is facility policy, you must shower twice a week with assistance. The times will vary depending on the availability of the nurse's aide. You will have two physical therapy sessions every day, seven days a week. Lastly, you will have one speech therapy daily for five days out of the week."

"Oh..."

"I know it's a lot, but these are the steps we need to take for you to regain your strength. The entire reason you're here is for rehabilitation, and we're going to do our best to get you back home."

The nurse went on to discuss goal setting and how through that we would be able to see the progress I would hopefully make. "By the end of your stay, we want you to be safely walking with a walker."

I nodded in response. I still had difficulty talking, so it was mostly a one-sided conversation. But I understood the plan laid out in front of me, and I felt a newfound determination to lift myself from how far I had fallen.

I stayed in the room for the rest of the evening. I was served dinner in bed, and once my meal was over, the nurse's aide helped me get ready for sleep.

❖   ❖   ❖

THE NEXT DAY I woke bright and early at 5 am, just as the nurse had promised. I was given medication and two hours later was brought breakfast. At around 9 am, the physical therapist came to meet me for our first session. She was a pleasant young woman with a bubbly demeanor. She energetically introduced herself and followed her introduction with words of encouragement, "We are going to do the very best we can to get you moving independently again!"

After our introduction, she helped me get from my bed into the wheelchair. She rolled me out of my room through the corridors to the physical therapy room. Before we began any exercises, she made sure to preface our sessions with words of heeding encouragement, "You need to know that this will be a slow process. It starts with you in your wheelchair, but eventually, we want you to be able to use a walker to get around."

She then went on to show me the different exercises I would do. I started out with a pulley attached to my legs that I was able to regulate. I had to lift my legs up and down, fighting the resistance of the pulley each time. Every exercise lasted 15 minutes. These exercises were overall fairly simple movements, but for me, they proved extremely challenging. Whenever I felt my body shake under the pressure of the weight, or even just the movement, it was tangible evidence of how weak I had become. My shakiness could have easily discouraged me, but I was so tired of being discouraged.

Instead of falling back into the bottomless pit I had fallen in before, I gave it my all and pushed to get better. Each sign of weakness was a chance to get better. And this time, I felt ready.

In addition to my physical weakness, I had difficulty remembering words. Speech therapy was done in my room to recuperate my vocabulary. The therapist would show me flashcards with different words on them. I had to pronounce simple vowels and words to build up my vocabulary. As we progressed, we would move on to whole sentences. It was all highly challenging for me. I couldn't think of words, nonetheless sentences, so I looked forward to the therapy helping me regain my mind. I also had occupational therapy to learn how to bathe, dress, cook safely and get in and out of a car's passenger seat.

Outside of my multiple therapies, I spent a lot of time on the quad patio. The building was square-shaped and in the middle was a spacious patio. I would hang out there every day for at *least* 15 minutes to take in some fresh air and soak up some sun. In the evenings we were allowed to meet visitors on the patio. I made plans with my friends for them to come to visit me. Each said they would bring me something—either magazines or a candy treat. This facility was much closer to my hometown, which is why so many of my friends and family agreed to see me. My daughter even promised she'd come by with my grandsons. I had so much to look forward to.

I felt as though I was in good hands. Finally, I was getting the proper help I needed. And finally, I no longer felt an impending sense of hopelessness around the next corner. Instead, I could feel hope grow with each step along the way.

The therapy department provided me with excellent care during my stay. As time went on in the facility, all the therapies were helping me build up my physical and mental endurance. I felt myself get stronger. I progressed to showering daily using a shower chair, I was able to transfer from my bed to my wheelchair all alone, and I graduated to using a walker periodically with supervision.

CHAPTER 12

Home Sweet Home

As MY DISCHARGE DATE drew near, a patient care conference was held to determine the best course of action
for my post-discharge care. Attending the conference
was a social worker, a therapist, a nurse, myself, and
my daughter who participated via conference call
on the telephone. The staff and my daughter agreed
I could only be discharged with continued physical
therapy and a caretaker. My daughter was not available to help me once I was home, so the only option
was to hire a private pay caretaker to help me.

We made a discharge plan to have a visiting nurse evaluate me before my physical therapist came to work on rehabilitation exercises. In addition to the visiting nurse and physical therapist, we planned to hire a home care assistant to help me with my daily activities. I agreed to all the discharge plans. The alternative discussed at the care conference was to sell my house and move into assisted living—an option I refused to consider.

While in the skilled nursing facility, I interviewed several healthcare workers for the role. I interviewed three different companies over the phone. Ultimately, I hired a lovely and compassionate lady who sounded soft-spoken. Her company charged $25 per hour for her services, all of which came directly out of my pocket. My health insurance plans did not cover any percentage of the service despite it being a necessity.

With a solid discharge plan in place, the rest of my time at the rehabilitation facility flew by. While still somewhat weak, I mastered the art of walking safely with a walker which was the intended goal from the beginning of my stay at the rehabilitation facility. I was released to go home on October 25, 2018, three weeks after admission.

Leaving this facility was much different than my departure from the psychiatric facility. With the assistance of my walker and a nurse's aide, I walked out to catch my ride, a non-emergency healthcare van. The van had accommodations for the new equipment I carried with me, and it was a pleasantly short drive to a town I was familiar with. The driver wasn't too chatty, he kept to himself mostly, but I didn't mind because my eyes were glued to the window, or rather, what lay beyond the window. I was excited to get home, and this time, I didn't feel alone.

After a long trip, there's nothing quite like the warm welcome of a familiar place. When we pulled into my driveway, I let out a sigh of relief. Granted, I was weak and still not myself, neither physically nor mentally, but I had a support system in place to help get me back to where I once was.

Next to us in the driveway was my caretaker waiting in her car. Once she saw us pull in, she exited her vehicle and came to help me inside. It was my first time meeting her in person since previously we had just talked on the phone. She was a woman from Fiji in her 30s and had been doing homecare assistance for a couple of years. She stood at an average height with long black hair tied in a bun, equally dark eyes that glinted when she smiled, and a wonderfully gentle and quiet demeanor.

Once inside, we made our way to my dining room table to review the terms of our contract. As we passed through my house, I saw all the mess I had left behind. The kitchen was cluttered with loose dishes and dirty towels, the sink was filled with dirty pots and pans, the dishwasher was full and not yet run through, and my garbage cans were filled to the brim. The house was in disarray. Despite the mess, I was happy to be home.

My caretaker was set to come eight hours per day for seven days out of the week. She would be in charge of fixing my meals, doing light housework, grocery shopping, washing and folding laundry, and assisting me with showering and dressing. I had some lingering confusion and forgetfulness, so she was also in charge of reminding me when to take my prescribed medications. Daily, she would leave me with a prepared dinner that I only had to heat in the microwave.

She reminded me not to shower without her, not to walk without my walker, and to take my medication. Even though she wasn't set to begin work until the next day, she prepared a bowl of soup for me before she left.

We wrapped up our business talk and she left to get some rest before beginning her role as my caretaker. Once she was gone, I ate my soup and went straight to bed. I was exhausted from the past three weeks, and I couldn't wait to sleep in my own bed.

❖   ❖   ❖

THE DAY AFTER I got home, a visiting nurse came to my house. Her assessment was done before the physical therapist's arrival to ensure I was physically fit to do all the required exercises. The nurse planned to come weekly to pour all my prescribed medications for the following week. This completely removed the possibility I'd make a mistake with my medication.

I was eager to continue building my strength and improving my walker skills, both indoors and eventually outdoors. Physical therapy started the day after the visiting nurse came and continued twice weekly. I was fully cooperative with all aspects of the care plan.

Because of my high blood pressure history, the physical therapist always took my blood pressure before starting therapy. About two weeks after I got home, per usual protocol, the therapist took my blood pressure. His eyebrows shot up with surprise and quickly furrowed together displaying concern. I knew the reading wasn't good. Not only was it very high at 190/130, but I simultaneously developed numbness on my right side and a severe headache. He immediately called 911. For context, a normal blood pressure range is near 120/80. My blood pressure was dangerously high.

An ambulance arrived within minutes. I was immediately given an intravenous (IV) in my left arm. This was considered a true emergency, so the first responders had the siren going to get us to the hospital as quickly as possible. I'm sure you've seen and heard emergency response vehicles speed down the road with their sirens on, but if you've never been in the back of one, let me tell you, it is LOUD. To make matters worse, the first responders checked my blood pressure every 30 seconds, and it was only going higher. The numbness and headache increased as well. I heard one of the first responders talking through a radio, notifying the hospital to prepare for my arrival.

As soon as we pulled up to the ambulance unloading dock, I was immediately rushed to a room on a stretcher. Staff circled me like vultures, ready to draw my blood, administer an EKG, start another IV, hook me up to a blood pressure monitor, measure my heart rate—*everything*. It was all completed within what felt like three minutes after my arrival. Even though every action was swift and there was a rushed tone in the room, everyone explained what they were doing to me and why they were doing it as they went along.

Amidst all the hustle and bustle, the doctor was able to complete an assessment. Once the assessment was complete, labs were drawn, x-rays were taken, and intravenous drugs were given, my blood pressure finally went down. The doctor told me I had a small stroke. They decided to hospitalize me to monitor and stabilize my blood pressure and the effects of the new medication.

Here I was, back in a hospital *again*—my fifth hospitalization in *five months*! I was once again terrified of never recuperating from all this. My mental health was still fragile, and now my medical health quickly matched it. I felt anxiety bubble inside my chest just thinking how far I was from my previous life of stability. After all my hard work in the rehabilitation facility, I was terrified that I'd never fully heal again. It was as if I had jumped into a deep pool with two large weights tied to my ankles, one being my mental health, the other my physical health. Together, they pulled me back into plummeting desperation.

Throughout all the 2018 turmoil of multiple hospitalizations, I constantly recited the Serenity Prayer —one of the go-to prayers of Alcoholics Anonymous. It helped me to 'stay in the day' and try to focus on 'one day at a time.' It was the best I could manage during such difficult times.

So after getting the bad news that I had suffered a stroke, I turned to the one thing I held constant: my faith.

God... Grant me the serenity to accept the things I cannot change, courage to change the things I can, and wisdom to know the difference.

❖   ❖   ❖

AFTER TWO DAYS IN the hospital, my blood pressure stabilized, and I was discharged home. I reinstated all my previous arrangements with my caretaker, the therapist, and the nurse. Once again, I was in my own home. I didn't have the same enthusiasm I had after leaving the rehabilitation center. Worn out from all my hospitalizations, I was reluctant to feel hopeful.

During this phase, I realized I wasn't used to being on the receiving end of caretaking, it was a new experience for me. As a nurse for over 50 years, it was familiar for me to be the caretaker, not the 'caretakee.' My caretaker encouraged me to relax, slow down, accept help, and continue to have hope. Having a daily caretaker was a very comforting experience. She was a gentle soul who provided genuine care from her heart.

After six weeks, I progressed with therapy, required less assistance with daily living activities, and safely walked outside with a walker. This progress reduced my caretaker's hours to four hours a day, my therapist to once a week, and total completion of the nurse's care.

Once the visiting nurse's time was over, a dear nurse friend of mine came once a week to pour my weekly-prescribed medications. I will always be grateful for her caring help in my time of need.

After about three weeks of her services, I heard of a mail-away pharmacy that labeled and prepackaged patients' prescribed medications each day. Mailing a month at a time, each medication was named and the dose was listed along with the date and time to take the medication. This service eliminates any possibility of making a mistake with dosing due to confusion, lack of attention, or whatever the reason may be. It was a godsend.

Since I was now home from the hospital and becoming more medically stable, I continued regular visits with my psychiatrist. I was still without a car and unable to drive, so I kept using Lyft to get to and from his office. My psychiatrist was 45 miles away from my house, and the trip cost me $40 each way.

My physical condition dictated that I would not be able to drive in the foreseeable future.

The $80 round trip fees were adding up, so I decided I needed to find a psychiatrist closer to home. A friend recommended a gerontology psychiatrist located eight miles from my house. I started seeing her in December of 2018.

My initial visit with her for a psychiatric evaluation lasted over one hour. She reviewed my medications and, for the time being, made no changes. She listened and eventually recommended I see a therapist who was part of her team.

During my first meeting with the new psychiatrist, she reminded me I was doing very well considering the trauma I had experienced.

Trauma.

That was the first time this word had ever been used to describe my situation. It's the first time I have ever even heard myself and the word 'trauma' used in the same sentence.

"What do you mean by trauma?"

She responded, "All 2018, you experienced cumulative traumatic experiences beyond your control. Along with everything else, you are suffering from PTSD."

That was when the past year flashed through my mind in an entirely new light. The five cumulative hospitalizations, being left in the ER hallway for 12 hours, being shipped in the middle of the night to a hospital 100 miles away, held on a 5150, the side effects to the lithium toxicity, being discharged too soon, having no mental health care support plan in place, the entire psychiatric experience, having a minor stroke, the solitude, the depression.

It all clicked.

CHAPTER 13

The Long Road Back

OVER THE NEXT TWELVE to fifteen months, my main job was to stabilize and heal. I was still coming to terms with the fact that I had been traumatized. It was all challenging for me to understand. I had never experienced such an unstable period in my life. The emotional bankruptcy I felt left me with absolutely no self-confidence. I was eager to heal my deeply wounded soul, but it was a painfully slow process.

Working with the new psychiatrist was a Godsend. She helped me put my experiences in perspective to better understand why my mind and body were reacting in the ways that they were. She explained that posttraumatic stress disorder is a type of anxiety disorder that can happen after a deeply threatening or scary event. People with PTSD can have insomnia, flashbacks, low self-esteem, and a lot of painful and unpleasant emotions. It may feel like you'll never get your life back. But it can be treated. She recommended I get a referral for short-term psychotherapy.

Trusting her judgment, I agreed to weekly therapy visits. I agreed because I was still depressed and full of fear. I was experiencing nightmares, insomnia, and a lack of appetite. I was avoiding friends and family. I felt like a failure and wasn't sure if I would ever return to my life as it was before my breakdown. I knew if I were left on my own again, things could somehow get worse.

I was set to meet with the therapist for the next six to eight months. She called the process we would

be going through together cognitive behavior therapy. The idea, she said, "is to change the thought patterns that are disturbing your life about your trauma
by concentrating on where your fears came from.
Together we will improve your symptoms, teach you
skills to deal with it, and restore your self-esteem."

I was trying to be an active participant in every
aspect of my life on a daily basis. During my therapy
sessions, I shared how alone I felt and the fears that
were still a big part of my life; however, I found myself face-to-face with my fears, and they were scar-
ing me into submission. They made me feel unsafe
at times with this new therapist. I was reluctant to
admit these feelings to her, but once I did, she assured me that it was normal to feel such a way, *especially* since I had been mistreated multiple times
in settings meant to better my health. Beyond our
meetings, many days I found myself unable to follow
through with exercise, eat healthily, or socialize. I felt

afraid even at my weekly home group AA meeting—a meeting that I had attended for more than *15 years*. I felt unsafe.

When the subject of unease was brought up in our meetings, the therapist helped me understand why I couldn't shake these feelings. She explained that part of PTSD is feeling unsafe and unsure about yourself and your surroundings. It can cause a strong sense of distrust towards everything. The safest way to overcome it is to process the trauma—to go back, reflect on all the experiences and instances that invoke said fear and trauma, and face them head-on in a controlled environment. No matter the quality of safety provided by the therapist, I was still uneasy about revisiting my trauma. I still had feelings of distrust which caused this process to take quite a while.

Over time, the therapist helped me consider things beyond my control. She helped me move forward by listening and reframing my experience. She used techniques like talk therapy, EMDR (eye movement desensitization and reprocessing), relaxation techniques, and deep breathing techniques.

She also recommended I return to meditation and physical exercise that I once incorporated into my daily life. On the topic of reflecting on things I used to implement in my life daily, I ended up (on many occasions) talking about my AA meetings. I am a huge advocate for AA. It was such a pivotal part of my life that I continued to attend meetings regularly. I mentioned to my therapist the many slogans we had in AA and how they helped me through many difficult times. Some of the most important ones for me were: 'one day at a time,' 'put one foot in front of the other,' 'let go and let God,' and 'just do the footwork and stay out of the outcome.' My therapist made note of these and encouraged me to continue using them. She said they were wonderful tools. They helped me recover once, and they can help me recover again, despite it being in a different context.

Each day I tried to do the best for myself to continue my healing. Some days were better than others, and many days I struggled and fell behind, but this was all part of my long journey back to stability. Despite the challenges I faced, I continued on my journey to mental health by implementing the different tools I had been given along the way.

2019 and 2020 were years of rebuilding my mental, physical and spiritual health. Truth be told, I had no idea how long it would take me to get back to normal. I look back now and realize it took over two years before I could say, "I'm back."

I began to experience improved mental stability thanks to my prescribed psychiatric medications, my health care team members, and my loving and supportive family and friends. Slowly but steadily, I became more reliable with daily self-commitments to exercise regularly, eat healthier, and socialize more. Adventuring out into the social world, my support system consisted of only those who knew about my breakdown and were loving and supportive throughout all my difficulties. A huge lesson I learned throughout all my difficulties and healing is that the rebuilding and healing of my whole life is not a solitary task.

PART TWO

CHAPTER 14

Breaking the Ice

N OW THAT YOU'VE EXPERIENCED the most tumultuous depressive episode of my life, allow me to properly introduce myself. Hi, I'm Mary. I'm a Mom, a Nana, a retired nurse, a recovering alcoholic, and I suffer from bipolar depression.

I'm doing much better today in the year 2022. I no longer struggle with daily activities, I have a zest for life, and am able to find value in deep connections to those around me. I'm active in my mental health recovery, and the results are astounding. I look and feel better than ever, and my relationships are flourishing.

The pandemic was a rocky time to be healing mentally. Much of my socialization in 2019 and 2020 was through telephone and zoom. To set myself up for success, I made sure to have a well-developed 'care team.' I included some friends, family members, and my psychiatrist to be on my team, all looking out for my wellbeing. Being on my team means they have permission to inform me of any changes in my behavior that concerns them. So far, none of them have observed any serious changes.

Once a sufficient amount of time had separated me from all my traumas of 2018, I was finally able to reflect on all that had happened:

- Having been placed on a 5150 hold as a danger to myself.

- Committed to a behavioral mental healthcare facility over 100 miles away from my home, family, and friends.

- Discharged after seven days while still mentally fragile and unprepared.

- Hospitalized in a general acute care hospital for lithium toxicity and other serious medical and neurological complications.

- Admitted to a skilled nursing facility for intensive rehabilitation to learn to walk again and improve my talking.

- Upon discharge, unable to care for myself at home, had to hire a caretaker.

- Having a stroke.

- Having to find a new psychiatrist.

- Developing serious side effects from one of the psychiatric drugs used in my treatment and having to take another drug to treat the side effect of involuntary mouth and tongue movements. (This side effect still has not gone away. It may never go away.)

- Experiencing PTSD.

NOTHING COULD HAVE PREPARED me for the events that transpired. I was fortunate to have the luxury of a supportive care team to help me through those dark days. The thought of having no one to fall back on in my time of need saddens me because of how difficult it already is to go through mental health struggles. I don't know if I would've been able to do it alone.

Another realization I had was the lack of care I received from my healthcare providers. Much of my dismay and trauma were caused by the healthcare facilities after I reached out for help. I didn't expect that to be the case. It had never occurred to me that I wouldn't be treated with respect and dignity in the mental healthcare system for a few reasons. One, because I was a nurse for 60 years and could never imagine doing what was done to me to any of my patients. Two, my years of experience led me to have faith in the healthcare system. And three, I had two excellent insurance policies.

This realization led me to ask questions like, why was I treated the way I was? Is this a new norm in healthcare, or was my case an exception? These questions pushed me to dig a little and do some research. My experiences and subsequent research made me aware that our mental healthcare system is broken.

In my research, I found limited access to services, limited personnel for services, and limited resources to be the new norm. I was amazed to learn how much is spent on healthcare nationwide, yet these practices continue to escalate. The amount of money spent on mental health treatment and services reached $225 billion in 2019, a number which was up 52% since 2009.[9] Prices will only continue to escalate.

My focus for the remainder of this book is to analyze my experiences as a mental health patient within the system while exploring these questions through a nurse's lens. We will address why U.S. healthcare prices are so outrageous, why there is a decrease in the quality of care, and what we can do to combat the constant increase in prices. Before we can delve into these issues, however, it is important to understand more of my personal story, specifically my relationship with alcohol and mental health throughout my life. So let's start back at the beginning, where it all began.

CHAPTER 15

Where it all Began

I WAS THE FIFTH of eleven children born into a Boston Irish Catholic family. I was the second of seven daughters and sister of four brothers. We were renters in a fourplex flat in Cambridge. My mother always told me it was an upscale neighborhood compared to the housing projects. It was a three-bedroom, one-bath railroad flat. It was not considered a railroad flat because it was near the railroad, but because of the long hallway that went from the front door to the back door, and all the rooms were directly attached to the hallway. My mother always described our neighborhood as three blocks from Harvard. There was only one small park around the corner from where we lived. It was paved in cement and was locked at 5:00 pm. Our real playground was playing in the Harvard Yards, where there was grass, stairs, and statues.

My first exposure to alcoholism came first-hand back when I was a child. It was a prominent part of my childhood because my father was an alcoholic. In my family, the needs of the individuals came secondary to the problems resulting from the alcoholic. Our family dream was for Dad to stop drinking. If only he stopped, everything would be fine.

We never talked about his drinking with each other, we all just learned to live with it. I don't remember even talking to my close friends about it in my teens. My experience taught me it truly is a contagious disease which infects all the family for the rest of our lives.

To love my father, I felt I had to ignore him. I ignored him and his drunken actions. However, despite my best efforts to ignore, I ended up resenting his drinking. This ultimately led to a complete lack of respect for him. My resentment was one of the emotional scars I carried with me for a long time. Unaware, everyone in the family was emotionally sick. This is part of the destructive force that alcoholism has on families.

Interestingly enough, in 1959, at 18, I was a student nurse in a city hospital in the Boston area where many of the patients were alcoholics, hospitalized for one reason or another. I was able to develop compassion for them and eventually even some compassion for my father. By then, I was no longer living at home but resided in the nurse's residence at the hospital. This gave me less exposure to his daily drinking, more exposure to others suffering from the same condition, and in turn, sympathy for my father.

The American Medical Association (AMA) didn't accept alcoholism as a disease until 1956. I was in nurses training from 1958-1961, and I'm not sure if the city hospital treated alcoholics any differently with this acknowledgment that alcoholism was, in fact, a disease. Nonetheless, we treated alcoholics of all ages, backgrounds, and in all stages of their disease, from mild tremors and nervousness to delirium tremens and the final stages of cirrhosis of the liver. People came in from all walks of life, from the heavy long-term drinkers to the young men and women just beginning to have medical problems associated with their drinking. Thinking back, I don't remember hearing anything about Alcoholics Anonymous (AA) as a student nurse. Still, AA was founded in 1935, 13 years before I had begun my nurse's training.

My father would later die a very tragic death from alcoholism at age 61. He passed out with a lit cigarette in an overstuffed chair in the family room.

WHERE IT ALL BEGAN

He suffered severe burns. He had to be airlifted to the Mass General Hospital Burn Unit where he died a day later.

I was sorry I didn't understand his struggle. I was sorry he died the way he did. I was sorry I didn't understand *alcoholism.*

Based on my childhood exposure to alcoholism, I swore, "As God is my judge, I will never let that happen to me." That, of course, did not turn out to be the case. In my early 40s, I was in a therapy group for adult children of alcoholics. Part of the therapy was reading a book by Claudia Black, Ph.D., entitled *It Will Never Happen to Me.* There is a line spoken by all who have been raised in a family where one or both parents have a problem with alcohol or drugs. She writes, "In alcoholic families most children move through adolescence appearing to survive the problems and hardships of life. They abide by the family rules: 'Don't tell–don't trust–don't feel' As resilient as children are, their survival techniques frequently contribute to a variety of problems in adulthood among them depression, inability to maintain intimate relationships, marrying an alcoholic/addict, or becoming an alcoholic/addict." While recognizing alcohol as the primary addiction within families, this book broadens the concepts to include addictive disorders such as other drugs, money-related addictions, food disorders, relationships, sex, and work addictions. It expands upon family rules and roles, family violence, and shame. Reading this book validated many of the scars I had from growing up with an alcoholic father. It was the first time I had seen my domestic situation in written word, describing the exact scenarios I went through and helping me understand the kinds of reactions and emotions I had growing up.

Author Janet G. Woititz wrote a book in 1983 entitled *Adult Children of Alcoholics*. She listed 13 characteristics most adult children of alcoholics have in common. I could identify with many of them:

1. Guess at what normal behavior is.

2. Difficulty following a project through from beginning to end.

3. Lie when it would be just as easy to tell the truth.

4. Judge themselves without mercy.

5. Have difficulty having fun.

6. Take themselves too seriously.

7. Difficulty with intimate relationships.

8. Overreact to changes over which they have no control.

9. Constantly seek approval and affirmation.

10. Usually feel that they are different from other people.

11. They are super responsible or super irresponsible.

12. Extremely loyal, even in the face of evidence that the loyalty is undeserved.

13. Are impulsive. They tend to lock themselves into a course of action without giving serious consideration to alternative behaviors and possible consequences. The impulsivity leads to confusion, self-loathing, and loss of control over their environment. In addition, they spend an excessive amount of energy cleaning up the mess.

I WAS OVERWHELMED WITH all this new information. Initially, I was in group therapy and was also referred to individual therapy to deal with my issues as an adult child of an alcoholic. Given a gentle and encouraging therapist, I was able to look at these issues, many of which had controlled my life, and grieve the loss of many aspects of my childhood. I stayed in therapy for eight years and walked through many dark passages, but eventually came out the other side. I will always be grateful to my therapist for teaching me to re-parent myself in a healthy way, to not live in the past, and to forgive my parents who did the best they could in a troubling time.

As Dr. Black states clearly in her book title, *It Will Never Happen to Me* is wishful thinking. To my surprise and dismay, it did happen to me. The progression of my alcoholism is well documented in the next chapter.

CHAPTER 16

Alcoholism as an Equal-Opportunity Destroyer

I DIDN'T START OUT as an alcoholic. My drinking for many years was that of a social drinker. I recall in my teens and young adult years I was so preoccupied and busy with attaining my life's goals and accomplishments that drinking was not an issue in my life.

After graduating from high school at age 17, I was busy preparing to enter a three-year nurse's training program to qualify for my state registered nurse examination. In the 50s and 60s, the main alternative to a five-year bachelor's degree in nursing was a three year residential nurse's training program in a hospital. Hospital-based programs were mainly focused on developing highly skilled nurses based on hands-on experiential learning. There were no 'associate of arts programs' nor were there junior colleges available to me at the time.

My nurse's training at a City Hospital was a demanding year-round program that sometimes worked us seven days a week, mostly evenings and nights, to fully staff the hospital wards. Throughout those three years, I was able to keep my eye focused on the prize, which was to graduate and become a registered nurse (RN). I was so focused on developing my nursing career that alcohol wasn't even on my radar.

After graduating from nurse's training and taking the State Boards in 1961, I stayed in the Boston area for a couple of years working as a registered nurse. But then, the old gypsy in my soul told me it was time to move away. Feeling uncomfortable in New England, I moved to New York City. In AA, this is called a "geographic." I, of course, blamed my move on the people, places, and things in New England for that uncomfortable feeling I had in my own skin. In AA, I would later learn we called it a case of the "RIDs" (restless, irritable, and discontent). I would also learn it was the beginning of my alcoholic thinking.

It was 1964, I was 23, and I loved New York City. I had the best job I ever had in my nursing career, and I was paid a great monthly salary. The Visiting Nurse Service of New York had a policy to give their nurses a one-month-a-year vacation to replenish themselves so as not to burn out.

I loved the city for all its diversity—the nightlife, the Broadway Theaters, the restaurants, Central Park, the museums, the dating—I just loved everything New York had to offer. I had found my home. I look back and realize how full of optimism I was. My perspective on life was that it was one big adventure, and I was invincible.

It was in NYC that I met the man I would marry. We dated for a couple of years, and by then, my drinking was more frequent because there were more dining out and celebratory occasions. I wasn't concerned with my drinking, I was still in the 'social drinker' category. I remember telling friends I had a cop on duty in my head when I was drinking, and he would let me know when I had enough. I thought all social drinkers had 'an on-duty cop.' I thought that was perfectly normal.

Initially I had a shared apartment in Upper Manhattan, the Washington Heights Section of Manhattan, but soon moved to East 63rd Street in the heart of the new single's district. I had a wonderful roommate from NYC who introduced me to more experiences in the city. I remember having so much energy and exuberance for life. The original TGIF Bar (Thank God It's Friday) was two doors up from the apartment building I lived in, and I found myself going there a couple of nights a week. Our doorman watched for me as I returned home each time.

I lived in NYC from 1964-1968. In January of 1968, the old familiar gypsy in my soul known as the RID's said it was time to leave NYC and move west to California. I again blamed everything around me for the unwelcome but familiar uncomfortable feeling in my own skin. This time it was because there were too many people in the city. "Another geographic," as we say in AA.

My husband-to-be and I moved to California and were married in 1969. In 1972 we were blessed with our daughter. The day I gave birth to her was the happiest day of my life. Becoming a mom was a major highlight in my life. The joy of watching her grow up is like no other joy I've experienced. She was such a good baby; she grew into an inquisitive young child and eventually matured into a caring and beautiful young lady. I was thrilled to witness all the stages of her life.

I never shared this with anyone at the time, but I was beginning to feel insecure as a mother. Even though I was friends with several other young mothers in the neighborhood, somehow, I couldn't share my insecurity. I felt guilty for even having those thoughts and feelings because in those days 'maternal instinct' was all you heard about. What if I didn't have that?

My drinking was becoming a small concern as my life became more complicated. I was a wife, mother, homemaker, nurse, and then a college student. The director of nursing at the hospital where I worked encouraged me to return to school and get my degree in nursing. She pointed out that my career would be limited if I didn't get a bachelor's degree. I enrolled as a freshman in the local junior college to begin my college experience.

I was in my 30s and was one of the oldest students on campus. None of my nursing experience or nurse's training counted, so I had to begin as a freshman. What I enjoyed most about college was I had to take all the non-nursing courses to meet my general education requirement. I learned so much in these classes, they really served to broaden my view of my world.

At this point, feeling more overwhelmed with all the roles I was playing, I found a glass of wine would calm me down. Rather than trying to solve the situation of too many demands in my life by letting go or asking the right people for help, I found wine helped ease the situation. In this phase of my drinking, I still considered myself a social drinker. Still functioning well in all frontiers of my life, I was happy for the time being. I worked part-time as a nurse and a student while maintaining full-time activities as a homemaker, wife, and mother. Friends admired me for my versatility, and I ate it up. I loved the recognition.

Over the next four years, however, my drinking progressed from social to problematic. During this time, I completed my Associate of Arts and bachelor's in nursing after attending college for a total of seven years. Though not yet a daily drinker, I still thought I was okay and could handle it. I thought an alcoholic was someone who drank daily, like my father. Most noticeable during these years were recurring problems in my marriage.

I was not aware of the progressive personality changes I was going through. I became angry more often, I was beginning to build up resentments towards people, discomfort in places, and disgust with things in my life. I was starting to minimize how often and how much I was drinking. Instead of one glass of wine, I would sometimes have two or three. I was moving closer to being a daily drinker. I remember telling myself, "I'm dancing as fast as I can to keep up." My expectation was still, "I SHOULD be able to do it all." I thought resentments were building because I wasn't getting help with the house chores and childcare. I became a vigilante, a lone rider picking up the slack of everyone around me. I blamed others for my mistakes, the disorganization in my life—for everything.

I could still juggle the daily demands of all my roles (being a wife, mother, nurse, and friend), but by age 38, my drinking was pretty much daily, and life's problems were mounting. My marriage began to fall apart, and within a year, we were divorced. We then began a long and painful fight over custody. One of my greatest regrets is that my daughter had to witness the irresponsible and dreadful behavior from both her parents.

My divorce only solidified my martyr mentality. I was disappointed that my life was falling apart, and of course, none of it was my fault. I began to develop a 'woe is me' attitude which quickly evolved into an unforgiving and judgmental attitude towards almost everyone in my life. "Poor me, poor me, pour me a drink" was now my go-to solution.

I never made the connection between the beginning of the turmoil in my life to the progression of my drinking. Divorced and now having joint custody of our daughter, my drinking only escalated. By age 43, drinking had become a part of my daily routine. The only time I realized alcohol was the problem was when I could not stop, even with the mounting consequences. I was a daily drinker, I was out of control, and I couldn't stop.

All I could think of was as a child I was told, "you're just like your father," and here I was years later, realizing it was true. My Dad was an alcoholic, and I, too, was burdened with this destructive disease. A disease that affected everyone it came in close contact with, especially those we love the most.

In the middle of my alcohol-induced fog, I made the decision to leave my profession as a nurse. I am very grateful I made that decision because my drinking only progressed. I left nursing and opened a flower shop in a seaside town in Santa Cruz County. My decision was not based on rational thinking or business planning but on my need to be in a place where I could drink daily, the way I then needed to, in order to feed the demands of my alcoholism. I justified all my alcoholic behaviors.

In those years, I made many irresponsible life decisions that created a lot of wreckage in my life—but more importantly, in my daughter's life. My daughter suffered the most from my active alcoholism. As my alcoholism progressed, her childhood was filled with uncertainty from her mother's decisions, just as my childhood had been from my father's alcoholism. I was now an undependable and irresponsible parent.

I was full of anger. Angry at the people in my life that caused me to drink. Angry at the places that provided me with alcohol. Angry at the alcohol because it had such a tight, controlling grip on my life. I was angry with GOD for making me an alcoholic. Now, more openly hostile to others and defensive with my self-righteous indignation, my drinking was none of their business.

Finally hitting bottom with my drinking, I was aware of the ravages that alcohol had in my life. I lost all my good friends and some family members. Drinking was no longer a social activity, but a solitary exercise to get me drunk and drown my woes.

I had heard about AA but didn't know what it entailed other than it was for alcoholics. If I went to an AA meeting, I must admit I was an alcoholic. I had never said those words about myself out loud. I was too afraid to go to AA for help. I was too afraid to admit that I needed help.

CHAPTER 17

My Name is Mary and I'm an Alcoholic

I COULDN'T PRETEND I was fine forever. I couldn't go on ignoring my life falling apart around me. I wanted to, but I couldn't. I waited until I was in total desperation, fully knowing I *needed* help, yet I still couldn't bring myself to go to AA. Doing so would admit failure. But I couldn't sit by and do nothing, so I opted to see a therapist instead. I found her in the Yellow Pages and booked an appointment. I learned later that she specialized in treating adult children of alcoholics.

My plan for therapy was to spend the time complaining about my childhood and my father's drinking. At the time I felt that he was the cause of my drinking. The therapist's agenda was much different. Less than halfway through our first session, she said she thought I had a problem with drinking and that I needed to start my therapy to focus on the real issue at hand: my drinking.

The plan she laid out for me was to stop drinking for 30 days, attend AA meetings daily, and see her once weekly. She was the one who started me on my journey to recovery, the first of what I later called a 'COINSIGOD' that happened in my recovery. Somehow, I had the willingness to do as she requested. Another 'COINSIGOD.'

I began to hold up my end of the plan I made with my therapist which was to attend daily AA meetings for 30 days and absolutely no drinking. I had no idea what I was in for that day, August 4, 1984, my first 24 hours without a drink, when I walked into my first AA meeting in Santa Cruz, California. Entering the rooms of Alcoholics Anonymous, I was petrified. When they asked the newcomers to introduce themselves, it was the first time I said out loud, "Hi, my name is Mary, and I am an alcoholic."

I couldn't stop crying. I cried for the next six months. Every time I said, "my name is Mary, and I am an alcoholic," out loud, I cried. Saying it forced me to face the reality that I indeed was an alcoholic. I cried because I spent my life saying alcohol would not destroy my adult life the way it destroyed my childhood. My best efforts couldn't change the fact that my drinking over the years went from social to problematic to alcoholic, and there was no going back.

How did it come to this? I was in a room filled with alcoholics, and I was one of them. Yet I was still in some denial that I was a 'real' alcoholic. Maybe my drinking just got a little out of hand. What if I stop for a while, would I once again be able to drink in moderation, like social drinkers? I wanted to continue seeing the therapist, so I kept my side of the bargain and went to daily meetings, didn't drink, took things 'one day at a time,' as we say in AA, and I did the best I could.

Attending daily meetings, I began to hear stories like mine from both men and women. I heard stories of progressive drinking, progressive problems, and the progressive loss of control. I started to identify. I began to feel hope. They spoke of abstinence from all alcohol, no moderation. They shared stories of the wreckage they caused in the lives of people they loved. They openly shared painful experiences. They shared the disappointments they had in themselves, their aspirations for a sober life, and how they're getting there 'one day at a time.'

I listened attentively to the heartfelt honesty I was hearing. After weeks of going to daily meetings, I told the therapist I, too, thought my drinking was a problem. Getting more comfortable and trusting in the meetings, I was eventually able to share my story. I recalled the wreckage of my past, the power alcohol had in my life choices, the damage I caused my daughter, and other harm I had done. I was able to speak honestly for the first time in a long time about my drinking. I was told to keep coming back and to remember our slogans: 'it's the first drink that gets you drunk,' 'let go and let God,' and 'one day at a time.'

I continued seeing my therapist, continued not drinking, and continued going to daily AA Meetings. Before I knew it, 'one day at a time' added up to a year of sobriety. In therapy, I learned that alcohol had played a major role in my choices over the years. It was a key component that led me into unhealthy relationships and unwise and irresponsible decisions that ultimately sent me deeper into my alcoholism. Alcohol also decreased my ability to be a functioning professional and caused me to leave my profession. Alcohol destroyed my ability to be a responsible mother and drove me to shun most of my parental responsibilities. Alcohol had *for years* directed my thinking, my decision-making, and my behavior.

My alcoholism wasn't just about the progression of my drinking, it was about the progression of creating many alcohol-related problems in my life, some of which will never be undone. My former ability to be a responsible and contributing mother, wife, friend, nurse, coworker, daughter, sister, and the like was lost in the progression of my drinking.

My alcoholism had taken away my life and gave me instead a very lonely and self-destructive existence. In AA, others who suffered similar consequences welcomed me. I was now home among a group of men and women from all different backgrounds, religions, jobs, sexual orientations, ethnicities, etc., who were joined by one common problem: alcoholism. At last, I was home. I was safe, hopeful, and willing. But most importantly, I was not alone.

I undid one of my "geographics" and moved back to Santa Clara County where I had previously lived for 16 years. I found that AA in Santa Clara was the same, if not better. It was full of people sharing a common bond of alcoholism who were willing to help other alcoholics get sober. I was welcomed by them and taken under their wings of unconditional love and unending encouragement. I was an active member of this AA community for the next ten years of my life. Here I built a strong foundation in recovery that included belief in a higher power, a God of my own understanding who loved me, taught me, guided me, forgave me, encouraged me, and had my back.

To learn the principles of AA and to solidify my early recovery commitment to sobriety, it was highly recommended that I get a sponsor to do the Twelve Step program. My first sponsor was chosen for me by other winners in the program. Winners are those who have long-term sobriety and help by mentoring people with less sobriety. They are respected elders in the program. Herself a winner with 20 years of recovery, my sponsor was a gentle and caring woman. Her guidance, wisdom, and encouragement walked me through the steps without fear.

Blessed with recovery, I kept from drinking 'one day at a time,' which eventually allowed me to return to my nursing career, repair my relationship with my daughter, and make amends to those I had harmed in my active drinking. Three years after getting sober, one of the amends I made was when I went to my father's grave and told him I was sorry he never got sober.

I went to his grave on a warm sunny day. I brought with me a packed lunch and a picture of my daughter. I sat and spoke out loud with him for about an hour and a half. I told him about my recovery and how much it had changed my life. I owned up to the bad attitude I had towards his alcoholism. I then showed him a picture of my daughter and said, "Dad, you would be very proud of your granddaughter."

CHAPTER 18

What Is Alcoholics Anonymous

A.A. HAS AN ESTIMATED worldwide membership of over two million people.[10] Founded in 1935 in Akron, Ohio, the newly sober Bill Wilson met the detoxing Dr. Bob Smith and put forth that alcoholism was not a failure of will or morals but an illness from which Wilson had recovered as a member of a Christian Revivalist Oxford Group.[11]

Dr. Bob and Wilson, the Co-founders of Alcoholics Anonymous, left the Christian group and designed the Twelve Steps of Alcoholics Anonymous. Substituting the Christian God with a "god of your own understanding," the pair implemented the concept of a more inclusive spiritual higher power which allowed people of all beliefs to come together. To this day, the concept of a "higher power of our own understanding" is practiced in A.A. all over the world. The only requirement to join A.A. is to have a desire to stop drinking.[12]

In 1939, Bill and Bob wrote and published *Alcoholics Anonymous: The Story of How More Than One Hundred Men Have Recovered from Alcoholism*. The book, referred to by members as "The Big Book," continues to be the solid rock foundation upon which our continued recovery is anchored. In 1946, the separate "Twelve Traditions" was added to formalize and unify the fellowship.[13] Alcoholics Anonymous was the original Twelve Step Recovery Program.

The American Medical Association (AMA) did not accept alcoholism as a disease until 1956.[14] This is amazing since Dr. Silkworth was instrumental in treating Bill Wilson, one of the founders in 1935, for alcoholism. Dr. Silkworth described alcoholics as having an allergy to alcohol. This allergy sets up an obsession and compulsion to drink more.

The Twelve Steps are intended as a non-coercive self-improvement program of admitting a lack of power over alcohol and its damage, striving to correct personal failings, making amends for past misdeeds, and continuous spiritual development while helping other alcoholics to stay sober through the steps. The steps introduce the healing aid of an "unspecified god as we understand him." Today I have completed my steps several times with my sponsors, and I believe it continues to be the road map to help guide me through life as a recovering alcoholic.

A.A. is self-supporting through voluntary contributions. The twelve traditions of A.A. informally
guide how individual groups function. There are no
leaders, we are but trusted servants. A member who
volunteers and accepts a service position typically
holds their position anywhere from three months to
two years. The time spent in their role is determined
by group vote and the nature of the position. A.A. is
maintained entirely through the willingness of volunteers and the contributions made by individuals in
the program.

The Big Book outlines the Twelve Steps philos-
ophy of recovery, which includes admitting a total
lack of power over alcohol and needing help from a
"higher power" to maintain sobriety as well as clean
up the wreckage of the past caused by our drinking.
Total abstinence one day at a time is a requirement
for continued recovery. All those who have relapsed
are always welcomed back to the fellowship. A.A.'s

program extends beyond abstaining from alcohol. Its goal is to change the thinking of an alcoholic to bring about recovery through a spiritual awakening.[15]

A.A. members practicing the Twelve Steps seek guidance and strength through several ways: prayer and meditation from the "god of our own understanding," daily moral inventory of resentments and thanks, listing and being ready to remove character defects, listing and making amends to those harmed, and trying to help other alcoholics. Recovery is about accepting responsibility for the damage to self and others in our life from our drinking and acknowledging the need to correct past personal failings and make amends for those we may have harmed along the way.

Learning and practicing the Twelve Steps to the best of our ability is done through the guidance of a sponsor who has done the steps and also practices them in their daily life. A sponsor should be the same sex as the sponsee, be an experienced fellow alcoholic, and refrain from imposing personal views on the sponsee. I have been blessed with several excellent sponsors in my 38 years of recovery. All have been loving and caring women who offered guidance in good times and bad. They provided me with the tools I needed in order to sponsor other women in the program.

CHAPTER 19

Double Trouble: Alcoholism and Mental Health

On August 4, 1984, I celebrated my first 24 hours of sobriety. A year and a half into my sobriety, I was hospitalized for severe clinical depression. Some say it was a miracle I didn't drink. Looking back, I believe I didn't drink because I fully accepted and understood that alcohol would not make me feel better. It was no longer the solution to my problem.

I was gifted with the ability to reach out to the right people to get the help I needed. A.A. treated my alcoholism, but I now had to depend on the medical community to treat my severe clinical depression.

Years later, I learned that one-third of alcoholics/addicts have a co-occurring disorder. In other words, a mental illness and substance use disorder that occur simultaneously. People with co-occurring disorders struggle to stay clean and sober until their mental illness is treated and stabilized[16], and they have a higher chance of being hospitalized than those with a mental health or substance abuse disorder alone.[17]

My mental health crisis transpired in 1986 and 2018, and I didn't drink throughout those difficult times. The common denominator during these times was my involvement in the A.A. Fellowship. Having a loving sponsor and a loving fellowship to support me through my mental health crisis is but one of the gifts of recovery.

I realize how blessed I am to have A.A. to treat my alcoholism and that I have the ability to advocate for myself in the mental healthcare system—two advantages many don't have. Despite these advantages and the fact that I spent an entire career in the medical workforce and the two excellent insurance policies I held, I was still mistreated. I was still taken advantage of. I was and still am a cash cow, and if you live in the U.S. and receive healthcare here, so are you.

CHAPTER 20

Faulty Faculties

I AM WELL INTO recovery from alcoholism, and thankfully, my journey in sobriety has been so successful that I am not tempted to drink on a daily basis. My time in A.A. has been one of the best choices of my life. Arguably an even better choice has been to stay involved in the A.A. community, help others reach sobriety, and maintain my own. It has been a long-term solution that's worked miraculously in my life and others' lives.

Alcoholism is considered a medical condition. As we've established, it involves frequent or excessive drinking regardless of the physical or mental problems piling up. But if alcoholism is a medical condition, why is it that the care I received within the A.A. fellowship has been some of the most effective and impactful care I've received throughout my entire life? Not to mention it's completely free.

The genuine care I saw and experienced within the A.A. community is unrivaled. A.A., being a self-supporting establishment and community, puts at its core purpose the desire to see those burdened with alcoholism become sober. It is founded on the desire and goal to help the well-being of as many people as they can. And it's clearly effective, since its beginning in 1935, A.A. has grown to have over two million members. What separates fellowships like A.A. from the United States healthcare system is how they view people–clients, patients, members, whatever you want to call them, it all comes down to the nature of how we are viewed. A.A. views alcoholics as people weighed down by a treatable disease, and this helps define their goals as rehabilitating alcoholics back into the world as highly functioning individuals.

On the other hand, the U.S. healthcare system has a much different perspective. Rather than receiving what we might expect when visiting a hospital (health-care, right?), we get increased treatment, decreased quality of care, and constantly increasing costs on ALL services, all under the guise of health care. This is because we are not viewed as people and patients who need long-term help but instead as sources of revenue. And the opportunity for money in an industry that oftentimes seems like the wild west is all too tempting for those at the receiving end of the checks. So they take advantage of us in many ways. We will only scratch the surface of the corruption in the United States healthcare system, but remember that it all comes down to our healthcare no longer prioritizing patient's best interest. Today, the healthcare system has become a big, big business.

I've told you the story of my success in seeking sobriety through A.A. and my hard-fought battle in the mental healthcare system. I've discussed the difference between the two and how I was able to thrive in one and not the other, but now I would like to look at each through the lens of my nursing expertise. When I was working through my mental health issues, I was unable to think clearly or rationally. My thinking was panicked and illogical. All my years as a nurse and the training drilled into my head were gone. I could not tap into my expertise, therefore, I could not see clearly the wrongdoings that were happening. But now, with a bit of time and therapy between the events that transpired, I can reflect back and see the rights and wrongs of the treatment I received.

In *An American Sickness,* Elizabeth Rosenthal lays out ten economic rules of the dysfunctional medical market. These rules do a great job of encapsulating the hectic medical market that exists today. I will use three of these rules to help frame my experiences. The three rules are:

1. More treatment is always better. Default to the most expensive option.

2. A lifetime of treatment is preferable to a cure.

3. There is no free choice. Patients are stuck.

WITH THESE RULES LAID out, let's take a closer look at my experiences.

EMERGENCY ROOM

MY INITIAL ADMISSION TO the hospital led me to experience things as a patient that I never would have imagined doing as a nurse. Upon admission and a brief meeting with medical staff, I was placed on a stretcher and left in the hall. At the time, I was afraid, so it was natural for my mind to explain away why they did these things. I justified it as, "Oh, the rooms are probably filled with heart attack and stroke patients since it's common practice to prioritize them." But how about the fact that I was under the supervision of a security guard? For this, I wondered what the staffing ratio was. It must've been high; they must have been very short-staffed to have a security guard observing a psychiatric suicidal patient instead of a more appropriate nurse or nurse's aide. Details like these add up, and in the moment, it's difficult to recognize the wrongdoings of these choices, but they are impactful.

Let's take a look at my medical chart from my trip to the hospital:

MEDICAL HISTORY AND PHYSICAL

DATE AND TIME

June 19, 2018, 3:44 pm

SOURCE

History is obtained from patient

HISTORY OF PRESENT ILLNESS

Patient is a 77-year-old female with history of high blood pressure and depression who presents for a psychiatric evaluation today. Patient reports that her psychiatrist advised that she come to the Emergency Department due to her worsening depression symptoms, which have been constant for six days. Patient doesn't feel safe at home, and a note that she has suicidal ideation with no set plan but states that she has thought of possibly overdosing on multiple medications. Patient states that she lives alone and only eats peanut butter and jelly sandwiches three times a day. Symptoms are described in moderate severity.

MEDICAL HISTORY

She has a past medical history of Anxiety state, unspecified; Depressive Disorder, not elsewhere classified; Hypertension Essential; and Unspecified Hypothyroidism. Other than high blood pressure, with a reading of 168/88, this pleasant female was in no apparent distress.

I WOULD LIKE TO point out a few things from this chart that should ring a few alarm bells. First, it is mentioned above that I live alone. A patient suffering from suicidal ideation that lives alone is an automatic trigger in identifying a patient as high-priority. Their age and whether they lived alone are two large factors in determining how quickly we must act to get them the care they need. In my case, I should have been identified as a high-priority patient who needed a developed care plan sooner than I was classified as such.

Further, the very last line of my report states, "...this pleasant female was in no apparent distress." No apparent distress? I was so terrified all I knew to do was to submit myself to the professionals whom I thought could help me—who I thought would keep my best interest in mind. Instead of being assisted and assured, I was laid on a stretcher in a high-traffic area observed by a security guard. I was already terrified before, but in those moments, laying in the hall, I was petrified. Being watched by a man in uniform enhanced my fear and made me feel needlessly guilty, as if I were a criminal. Those seeking help in a mental health crisis are already under extreme anxiety and doubt; putting them in such an unstable setting exacerbates the crisis even further. So, no, I was not a pleasant female in no apparent distress. I was a compliant suicidal patient in terrible crisis.

Rosenthal puts it best, "Doctors traditionally praised 'compliant' patients, individuals who did what they were told, followed instructions, and didn't ask too many questions. Medical journals used to publish profiling their opposite: 'difficult patients,' those who didn't just follow doctors' orders, who asked questions and expressed too many opinions." But as it stands in the medical world now, it is more beneficial for our health and wellbeing to be the "difficult patient." We must ask questions and demand explanations to be involved in the decision-making process of our own health.

Instead of receiving care in a timely manner, which is my right, I was left in the hallway on that stretcher for *12 hours*. 12 hours! That is simply preposterous! When has it become at all acceptable to leave anyone waiting that long, nonetheless an unstable psychiatric patient?

The law states that if you are a danger to yourself, your care providers must put you in a locked facility. The big issue in my case was that no mental health hospital beds were available nearby. The inpatient services for mental health patients are limited based on insurance company policies. After my own experience, I began to wonder how a metropolitan area with a population of over two and a half million people could have an inadequate number of psychiatric beds to meet the needs of the seven acute care hospitals in the area. Not included in the above statement are the endless number of psychiatrists and medical doctors also making referrals to the mental health system.

An insurance plan network (for example, health maintenance organizations or HMOs and preferred provider organizations or PPOs) can be made up of hospitals, doctors, and other health care providers/ facilities that have agreed to the negotiated terms of the plan. To understand HMOs and PPOs better, let's look at Medicare.

The establishment of Medicare on July 30, 1965, made the government the largest payer for healthcare services. Many providers from across the spectrum of healthcare then saw the government as a cash cow that they wanted to milk.

What happened next? Healthcare costs *skyrocketed.* In the 1980s, the U.S. spent around $247 billion on health care—an amount equal to 9.4% of the Gross National Product (GNP).[18] The solution to this financial catastrophe was the introduction of a managed care model for healthcare services that would save costs. The advent of managed care launched us into a new era of healthcare which introduced HMO's and PPO's.

The insurance industry became very powerful in making decisions about all patient care, including accessibility, quality, and costs. We see today that the determinant of quality and care are (for the most part) disregarded. In my specific case, the mental health institution's location was not based on geographic population needs but financial gain. The healthcare policies dictate where hospitals are to be built and where doctors are to practice, thus determining the lack of availability and accessibility of proper care. These are the reasons I would qualify my happenings at this initial hospital under "there is no free choice, patients are stuck" from Rosenthal's ten economic rules of the dysfunctional medical market. I had no choice in where I would be taken care of, and even if I had a say, there were limited options and limited availability (room and board) within those options. Thus, I was stuck. Stuck on that stretcher for 12 hours, stuck hitching a ride in an ambulance 2 hours away, stuck with egregious bills, and there was nothing I could do about it.

The average price for a trip to the emergency room is $3,000. The cost of an ambulance ride to Santa Rosa ranges anywhere from $1,200-2,100, not to mention there was an additional fee of $38 for every mile the way there. Since I was over 100 plus miles away, that meant *at least* an additional $3,800. Luckily, I have two excellent insurance plans that covered these hefty bills, but not everyone is as fortunate as me. And for those with great insurance coverage, have you ever looked at the bills your insurance pays? Not many people do (I didn't until I began writing this book), and there's no need to since the payments aren't coming out of your pocket, nor are the itemized bills sent to you unless otherwise requested. However, more of us should be checking these bills to be aware of the current costs of our treatment. The more aware we are, the better we can advocate for ourselves.

Out of sight, out of mind, is how the medical market has grown to be such an anomaly. We don't see the egregious prices or the drastic difference in price for the same treatment at different locations, but our insurance pays for it, making it barely a second thought in our minds. This is how we are tricked. We don't see the consistent increase in price, thus, we aren't even aware there is an issue until our insurance premiums increase the next year to make up for the costly coverage the years prior. In the end, we pay for these steep expenses. Hospitals and medical monopolies in the game raise their prices, insurance companies cooperate and pay those absurd prices, and it comes back around to us; all the while we have no idea *why* or *how* prices grew to what they are to-day. Asking questions and being involved in the decision-making process of our care is one way we can work to stay involved in the world that is our health-care.

SANTA ROSA HOSPITAL

BEFORE MY TWO-HOUR AMBULANCE ride to Santa Rosa, I was informed of my placement under the 5150 hold. Again, a 5150 hold allows a person deemed gravely disabled or a danger to others/themselves to be involuntarily detained in a locked facility for a 72-hour hospitalization for psychiatric evaluation. I think this was the right choice. It was a serious decision, but I was in a seriously dangerous state of mind, and my health was in jeopardy. It's a bit mind-boggling that they placed me under such a serious hold but left me to wait for their decision for 12 hours.

The other upsetting part of having been placed on a 5150 hold is that no behavioral mental health care facilities were available near me. There was only one in Santa Rosa, which was over 100 miles from home, family, friends, and everything I was familiar with. It was a big deal to be that far displaced from everything I knew and loved. This falls under the same Rosenthal rule of being stuck with no free will. Had there only been another local hospital with a mental facility (or two), this additional stress and cost could've been avoided.

Furthering the list of relevant happenings that fall under this rule, I also categorize my premature discharge from the mental facility under "there is no free choice, patients are stuck." I was discharged after a quick six-day stay. At the time I was still unquestionably mentally fragile, unprepared, and unfit to leave. This decision marked the inevitable decline in my overall health, not just my mental health.

Leaving prematurely was not my choice, it was decided for me. I believe the decision of my discharge was not based on individual patient needs but on profit expenditures. Because of the priority of profit expenditures, insurance can override the doctor's clinical assessment on whether or not a patient needs to extend their stay. If a person outwardly meets the minimum basic requirements for discharge (i.e., no longer suicidal but still in a horribly fragile state), they are more than likely to be discharged. The person making such a decision may not even be a medical professional. Regardless of who's making the decision, there are policies in place to get the patients in and out as soon as possible. Either way, the same issue remains of cost-efficient strategies overriding the well-being of the patient.

Nonetheless, I was released with no follow-up plan. Being ill-prepared upon my release left me confused and disoriented, and this lack of clarity led me to mix up my medicine dosage, landing me back in the hospital.

HOSPITALIZED FOR LITHIUM TOXICITY

NOT LONG AFTER MY week at the Santa Rosa hospital I was admitted to the acute care hospital for lithium toxicity, thyroid toxicity, poor nutrition, dehydration, acute renal failure, acute kidney injury, and acute metabolic encephalopathy. I was left on my own after discharge from the Santa Rosa hospital with no follow-up plans, no discharge notes, and no support. I essentially poisoned myself by messing up the dosage of medicine I was meant to take in my confused state. Although my misdosage and subsequent hospitalization could not have been planned, based on my mental state at the time, it was obvious that I was in no condition to properly care for myself. So, by releasing me when I clearly wasn't ready, it could have easily been predicted that some kind of complication would've happened. Thus, this falls under two rules: "more treatment is always better" and "a lifetime of treatment is preferable to a cure." My ongoing health issues led to further financial gain for the system.

From this general acute care hospital, I was admitted to a skilled nursing facility for intensive rehabilitation to learn to walk and talk again (the more treatment, the better!). But things finally turned around for the better at the rehabilitation center.

REHABILITATION CENTER
AND HOME CARE

I NOTICED A SIGNIFICANT difference in the care I received at the rehabilitation center. I came to them in an extremely weak state. I had lost the ability to speak, the ability to walk, and my physical health was still in jeopardy.

They had an intensive rehabilitation plan for me that consisted of multiple therapies daily. But the care didn't stop there. I felt as though the professionals working with me were genuinely invested in seeing me get better. They cared. I finally felt as though I had the adequate care I deserved.

Once my stay was nearly over, I had multiple meetings discussing my discharge with my patient care team, including my daughter. It was extremely thorough, and from it, we came up with a discharge plan designed to increase my odds of a continued successful recovery.

The plan consisted of having a private daily home care worker, a weekly physical therapist, a weekly RN, and pre-scheduled appointments to see my psychiatrist. I felt confident that I could heal. And then, of course, I had a small stroke. Unknown to me at the time, the stroke was a result of the compounding stress of all that I had gone through.

Luckily, I was with my physical therapist who caught it during our session. This goes to show that the treatment plan was extremely effective in looking out for my safety and well-being at home. I had multiple safety nets because had I not been with my physical therapist, I would've had my home care worker to call an ambulance. I hate to imagine what may have happened if I had been left alone like I was during my first discharge...

I had a total of five hospitalizations, three of which resulted from complications from the prior two healthcare facilities. All of this would again fall under the two rules of "more treatment is always better" and "a lifetime of treatment is preferable to a cure." In short, I needed a lot of treatment for my treatment.

LONG-LASTING EFFECTS

I STILL FACE SOME lasting effects that I continue to treat, the first being serious side effects from one of the psychiatric drugs, Latuda, used in my original treatment during the 5150 hold. The side effect is an involuntary movement of the mouth and tongue. This is treated by taking yet another pill (a very expensive one) to reduce the symptoms. These long-lasting effects are likely to be something I must deal with for the rest of my life.

The next lasting effect is my PTSD. This disorder has caused a permanent change in my thinking. Episodes can flare up from stress, anxiety, or paranoia. Often I may start to overthink what I've been through which causes me to become overwhelmed and fearful.

Aside from bouts of anxiety, PTSD has changed my sleeping habits, making it difficult to fall and stay asleep. I have had to make an overall lifestyle change. I no longer have caffeine as it is too strong of a stimulant for my brain and has the negative effect of increasing my stress levels. To calm down, I remember what I learned in therapy—I take deep breaths and refocus, say the serenity prayer out loud, and remember my tools.

Looking back on my care, I've concluded that had I been treated more intensively for my original psychiatric hospitalization (i.e., staying in the hospital after the suicidal ideation left me but I was still deeply depressed), a lot of medical complications could have been avoided. Had I stayed there and had more time to heal and gain more mental clarity, the complications I suffered would not have happened.

When I initially reached out for help in the ER, I was met with horrible attitudes from the emergency room staff while in a dire situation. Had I been met with genuine concern and care for my well-being, I may have avoided such a traumatizing experience.

And had I been spared these complications, lots of time and money would've been saved.

CHAPTER 21

Taking Action Towards Change

TODAY THE CONTINUED IMPLEMENTATION of managed care has not saved money as promised. Spending continues to grow. According to the Centers for Medicare & Medicaid Services, U.S. healthcare spending grew 9.7% in 2020, reaching $4.1 trillion. This means healthcare is responsible for 19.7% of the nation's Gross Domestic Product.[19] This amount includes $280 billion in spending on mental health care.[20] Even with increased spending on mental health treatment and services (52% spending increase since 2009[21]), access and treatment are still major issues.

Keep in mind that managed care's primary goal was to save money, yet the opposite continues to happen each year. With all this spending, why is it so difficult to get quality health care? What's happening to all aspects of providers that make healthcare so alien, confusing, and obscure to the average patient? A significant factor in the obscurity of the healthcare system has to do with the people that have become the new executives: administrative corporate businesspeople (extremely high-priced businesspeople, might I add). To expand the new corporate for-profit system, providers have integrated these businesspeople to reach their profit goals. It is no longer the front-line healthcare workers at the top of the food chain making administrative decisions; it's businesspeople. This means that each decision is strategic, meant to generate more money for the business.

Primary care providers (PCPs) are physicians as-signed to specific caseloads. A new role PCPs have is to keep costs down by limiting patient access to labs, x-rays, expensive radiology tests, and especial-ly medical specialist referrals and hospital admis-sions. Hospital beds and specialists are the costliest resources in the healthcare network, thus, access to them is closely monitored. Now known as 'gatekeep-ers,' our PCPs and others created in the new system have the job of making it more difficult for patients to access these costly services. The rewards for this service can be cash bonuses. Each decision made is a strategic one meant to generate more money for the business—from the restructuring of executive power to new procedures to follow, it is clear the system has morphed into a big business.

A few examples we've seen in my story include the location of hospitals, bed availability, staffing ra-tios, policies and procedures of care, and of course, charging for absolutely anything and everything. This last one actually falls directly under one of Rosenthal's rules of a dysfunctional market, one that I have not yet mentioned but is pertinent: "There are no standards for billing. There's money to be made for anything and everything."

For the first six months of this year, my insurance paid $33,322.40 for my prescription medication. This is especially troubling because my insurance has the power to negotiate prices and still my bill was astronomically high. Most of my drugs are generic with the exception of one expensive drug which costs $3,000 per month, of which I pay $50. This is yet another reason it is so important to start requesting your bills from insurance, even if it's not coming out of your pocket. What you may find are absurd charges that make no sense and seem pointless. They certainly have a point, however: to rake in cash.

In *An American Sickness,* Rosenthal eloquently lays out real-life stories of people who have been hurt by our healthcare. She uses these stories to expose the many flaws in our system and builds up to the ways in which we can push to make it for-patients as opposed to for-profit. I highly recommend you give her book a read. It is educational on the state of our healthcare.

If trends continue in an upward trajectory, national health spending is projected to reach $6.2 trillion by 2028.[22] That means the trend of paying more for less will continue as well. Mental illness affects tens of millions of people each year, yet it's estimated that only half of these people receive treatment for their illness.[23] In 2020 suicide was the 12th leading cause of death overall in the United States, claiming the lives of over 45,900 people.[24] With mental illness affecting as many people as it does and driving over

45,000 to end their lives, less will not do. We need more. We deserve more.

There are a few ways we can jumpstart the move towards change in our system. As we've established, our healthcare has evolved into a big business that seeks profit in every hidden corner. The best way to combat this is by gaining transparency. Transparency will allow us to determine for ourselves which care and prices are fair and ethical, and which are not. To achieve such transparency, we must become stronger advocates for ourselves.

There are many ways we can become stronger advocates. As I've mentioned before, we need to start asking our insurance companies to mail us an itemized breakdown of the bill our insurance company is paying. What this will do is reveal hidden and outrageous costs, which in turn will make us more likely to demand pricing before going through with future treatments/procedures. As of now, some hospitals refuse to provide this information, but if more and more patients demand it, they will have to reveal their pricing.

If we successfully pull this vital pricing information from hospitals, we will be able to compare and contrast prices from one healthcare facility to the next. Currently, there is no way to compare prices like you might when shopping for certain clothes or food. I can easily look up 'black boots' and compare ten similar boots with varying prices. I can just as easily run into my local grocery stores and compare the price of an organic bag of baby carrots to find the best deal. There is no such option when it comes to healthcare costs. I likely won't know how expensive something is until after I've received the treatment and am waiting for the bill.

This would begin a buildup of transparent data that patients can access, which will help us make educated financial decisions in our health care. The ideal end goal would be to have this data easily accessible with a quick call to the hospital or a quick search on the internet. This won't be easy, however. Big businesses *will not* want to give up their hidden prices. The fact that they are hidden is the reason they are able to continue charging so much. Once they're out in the open, it will be much harder for them to justify charging so much.

Another way we can push for change is by becoming more involved in local and national elections. We need our representatives to *represent* us and fight for healthcare reform. In order to know who's going to fight for us, we need to know who is getting lobbyist money from the healthcare industry. Because legislators get so much money from the healthcare lobbyists, it is a conflict of interest between representing the people and feeding their own greedy desires. We can combat this by demanding the release of how much they make from healthcare. To get what we rightfully deserve, we need to fight for across-the-board money transparency, locally and federally.

Lastly, one of the most important things we can do is talk. Change begins with knowledge about an issue, and not everyone knows how bad things have gotten. We need to bring this up much more to make it a national topic of conversation, otherwise, nothing will happen. Nothing will change as long as we remain idle.

CHAPTER 22

What My Life Is Like Today

It is now 2022 and four years since my psychiatric hospitalization in June 2018. My mental health recovery took over two years, a long time to fully heal and return to my true self. I was not prepared for how long it would take to stabilize mentally, but I really had no choice.

Unlike my previous experience of 1986, when my recovery was a matter of weeks, it took me much longer to heal due to the lack of adequate treatment I received. What helped me accept the long process

of healing was the encouragement from my psychiatrist, family, and close friends.

Today I am armed with many tools to help with
my ongoing healing and to help me continue to accept
my mental health diagnosis. I continue seeing my
psychiatrist regularly for medication management
and to reinforce the work done with my therapist,
who not only taught me healthier coping techniques
but also helped me to process the shame I felt about
my breakdown. I continue to mingle with select family and friends who give me encouragement and love
on a consistent basis. I am truly blessed to have a
healing and loving sponsor in A.A. who reminds me
regularly that God has my back. I have come to believe strongly that I need healthy people in my life to
also have my back.

In therapy, having learned as much as I could
about healthy self-care and developing tools to
change my thinking and behaviors, I now realize that

to continue to heal and get better, I also need my A.A. recovery tools more than ever. Over time, becoming more stable mentally, I have found I depend on my recovery tools from Alcoholics Anonymous (A.A.) every day for continued acceptance. My acceptance is more fluid than solid. On a good day, it is easy to accept I have bipolar and alcoholism; however, on a bad day, I could move back into anger or bargaining or even the 'poor MEs.' My A.A. tools remind me to 'accept life on life's terms,' to take things' one day at a time,' to be 'guided by a higher power' to 'do the next right thing,' and to 'do the footwork and let go of the outcome.' Using these tools and then some remind me I did not cause my alcoholism or my bipolar. I was, however, the only one who could ultimately pull myself out of these deep issues. Thus, I need to play an active role daily in the ongoing 'fix me project.'

I am the most important member of my healing team, just as you are the most important member of yours. If you happen to be struggling with any similar issues to mine, whether it be alcoholism or depression or bipolar, just know that you are not alone. You, too, can develop a healing support system. It may not be easy, but it is very attainable. There are people and communities around you who are there waiting for you to reach out. The most important word of advice I can give you is to not combat it alone. You are the most important part of your healing team, but you cannot be the only member. Find the courage to reach out, you deserve it.

If you happen to be blessed enough to not struggle with any of these afflictions, I challenge you to look at your own prejudice on addictions and mental illnesses and become willing to educate yourself properly on the illnesses of those around you. The fact that you've made it this far into my book means you've already begun that process of reeducation, so I would like to thank you.

At this point in my life, I am mentally stable and grateful to be fully restored. I don't take my mental health for granted. I am aware that my big job is to monitor my thinking and behavior on a daily basis and report any changes to my psychiatrist. It's a continuous process of recovery.

About a year and a half ago, I faced another depression. It frightened me, but I immediately spoke with my psychiatrist who added a new medication that treated the depression, and I am again stable. Every time I hit a bump in the road I return to thinking, "It's my fault, I did something wrong." I have learned to share this with my psychiatrist, who once again re-educates me about the brain's chemistry, and I am back on track.

Another acceptance I have to make on a daily basis is to accept that all psychiatric medications have side effects like drowsiness, dizziness, weight gain, dry mouth, constipation, nausea, vomiting, and of course, tardive dyskinesia. I pretty much feel medicated most of the time. The tradeoff for me is accepting the reality that I can live a full and healthy life with the help of medication, and *that* is my primary goal: a full and healthy life.

Today I have returned to being a high-functioning mother, sister, friend, nurse, and most of all, Nana. Daily I pray for continued mental, physical, and spiritual fitness to keep doing life the way I want. I have my sense of humor back and finally feel comfortable saying, "I am fully back."

It has been a long journey, and I didn't do it alone. I found the courage to persevere and not give up on myself. These past three years have changed my life. More than once over these years, I wasn't sure I would be restored to sanity. Losing my mind at age 78 was the most frightening experience of my life. Developing a trustworthy team of supporters has been paramount in my recovery.

Today, I continue with my trustworthy support team and add new people who enter my life. They are my guardian angels. It may sound trite, but some of the A.A. slogans that help me daily are 'one day at a time,' 'do the next right thing,' and 'let go of the outcome and do the footwork.' I follow directions from my doctors and continue to play a very active role in my continued healing. My psychiatrist sees me regularly to monitor my medication and support me emotionally. I am so happy I found her as she has had a profound effect on my mental health recovery. Even with stabilizing my mental health, I pay close attention to my daily moods.

I am aware that I have been able to advocate for myself, especially in the mental health care system, and I do not take any of that for granted. Many people cannot self-advocate or don't have a family member or a friend who will support and represent them. Many of them often fall through the cracks of the mental health system and don't get the services they need and deserve. I suggest they find an Ombudsman or a patient care advocate to assist them in getting the treatment they are entitled to under their patient rights.

My daughter, son-in-law, and three grandsons play a big part in my life once again. With their support and love, I am blessed. Living close to them, I play an active role in their lives, and they play an active role in mine, another big gift in my life and continued healing. It is such a wonderful role to be a Nana. I love them all to the moon and back.

Since sharing the details of my mental health crisis and my A.A. recovery, my friends and family on the East Coast have supported me in my journey. Because of this, I have become closer to my surviving three brothers and four sisters. In 2021 during the pandemic, I started a quarterly family zoom meeting. It is a delight to reconnect with the whole family, we even have nieces and nephews who join us. It's always a joyful reunion. Today, I have been able to share the terrifying experience I had as well as my healing and recovery with all family members.

I remain an active member in A.A., and on August 4, 2022, I celebrated 38 years of sobriety. It is truly a miracle. Even though my mental health recovery was a process that took over two years, I know I would not have survived without my daily dependence on my higher power, the God of my understanding, the Alcoholics Anonymous Fellowship, my meetings, my sponsor, and the Twelve Steps and Principles. In times of despair and doubt, I can talk with my sponsor and she would guide me back to today and remind me "to let go and let God." I also have used my zoom account to hold three A.A. meetings online weekly. It is such a gift to study the steps and traditions in a group of supporting people.

After a long hiatus, I have returned to my role as a nurse support group facilitator working with my nurses who struggle with alcohol, drugs, or their mental health. Having practiced as a registered nurse for over 60 years, supporting young R.N.s on their journey is an honor. Since 1997 I have conducted a weekly confidential one-hour group for R.N.'s who are willing to address their substance use disorder and/or mental health issues as it pertains to their professional and personal life. Discussions include addiction, recovery, relapse prevention, return to work issues, and ongoing daily activities to support recovery.

Most of all, I am so grateful for all those who play an active role in my recovery. I found the courage to write this book with their love and support. Admitting publicly that I have two diseases that caused me a lot of shame can be risky. I learned as a young child these are topics best not talked about. I recall voices from the past saying, "keep the family secrets in the family," and "what will the neighbors think?"

Today, I am guided by a different set of ideas. I am guided by a deep sense of responsibility to make my significant journey public not only to help my healing but to help others. In addition, an important part of my healing is telling my story and continuing to rid myself of shame. I also hope by sharing my personal experiences on the journey, I have provided new information that recovery from mental health and substance abuse is not only possible but also feasible for those of us afflicted.

My intent was to provide information on the mental healthcare system and how to navigate the system to get the services you need and deserve, to be a self-advocate or find someone to advocate for you, and to be aware that the "for-profit" healthcare system we have in America will only continue to grow unless we do something about it.

The questions to ponder are these: How can I begin to make changes in the way I participate in today's healthcare system? What are my patient rights and how can I fight for them? Know that every hospital has patient ombudsman services, whose job is to advocate for your care. These steps are a small beginning of the much-needed shift back to patient-centered care as opposed to our current for-profit business model.

I hope I have provided enough personal information about my dual diagnosis of mental health and substance abuse issues. I want to make people more aware that we have options. Those of us afflicted by substance abuse and a mental health diagnosis need to accept that our diseases have no cure, but on a daily basis we can play an active role in arresting them. Only we can comply with our medication regime to help us stabilize. Only we can eat healthier. Only we can find good friends to talk to when we are in need.

I want others to know that there is hope because what we have is treatable. We can learn what we have is not a failure or a weak-willed personality flaw or something to be ashamed of. I wish all afflicted would get the help they need, and I wish all those we love to continue to love and support us on our recovery journey.

REFERENCES

1 "Crisis and 5150 Process." *FERC*, Mental Health Association of Alameda County, https://ferc.org/crisis/#:~:-text=5150%20is%20the%20number%20of,for%20up%20to%2072%20hours.

2 "Health Insurance Portability and Accountability Act of 1996 (HIPAA)." *Centers for Disease Control and Prevention*, Centers for Disease Control and Prevention, 27 June 2022, https://www.cdc.gov/phlp/publications/topic/hipaa.html.

3 "Lithium Carbonate Oral: Uses, Side Effects, Interactions, Pictures, Warnings & Dosing." *WebMD*, WebMD, https://www.webmd.com/drugs/2/drug-5887-42/lithium-carbonate-oral/lithium-oral/details.

4 "Lurasidone (Latuda)." *NAMI*, National Alliance on Mental Illness, https://www.nami.org/About-Mental-Illness/Treatments/Mental-Health-Medications/Types-of-Medication/Lurasidone-(Latuda).

5 "Types of Bipolar Disorder: 1, 2, Mixed, Cyclothymic, and More." Edited by Jennifer Casarella, *WebMD*, WebMD, 20 Apr. 2021, https://www.webmd.com/bipolar-disorder/guide/bipolar-disorder-forms.

6 "Symptoms - Bipolar Disorder." *NHS Choices*, NHS, 14 Mar. 2019, https://www.nhs.uk/mental-health/conditions/bipolar-disorder/symptoms/.

7 Escamilla, Michael A, and Juan M Zavala. "Genetics of Bipolar Disorder." *Dialogues in Clinical Neuroscience*, Les Laboratoires Servier, 10 June 2008, https://www.ncbi.nlm.nih.gov/pmc/articles/PMC3181866/.

8 "Bipolar Disorder." *NAMI*, National Alliance on Mental Illness, https://www.nami.org/About-Mental-Illness/Mental-Health-Conditions/Bipolar-Disorder/Treatment.

9 "What You Need to Know about the Cost and Accessibility of Mental Health Care in America." *NAMI*, 10 May 2021, https://www.nami.org/Press-Media/In-The-News/2021/What-you-need-to-know-about-the-cost-and-accessibility-of-mental-health-care-in-America?feed=In-the-news.

10 Alcoholics Anonymous (April 2016). "Estimates of A.A. Groups and Members As of December 31, 2020" (PDF). Retrieved 17 December 2016. cf. Alcoholics Anonymous (2001). Alcoholics Anonymous (PDF) (4th ed.). Alcoholics Anonymous World Services. p. xxiii. Retrieved 17 December 2016.

11 Stevens, John W. "Bill W. of Alcoholics Anonymous Dies." *The New York Times*, The New York Times, 26 Jan. 1971, https://www.nytimes.com/1971/01/26/archives/bill-w-of-alcoholics-anonymous-dies-bill-w-oi-alcoholics-anonymous.html.

12 *"Pass It on": The Story of Bill Wilson and How the A.A. Message Reached the World.* Alcoholics Anonymous World Services, 1984.

13 "The Twelve Traditions." *Alcoholics Anonymous*, https://www.aa.org/the-twelve-traditions.

14 "Is Addiction Really a Disease?" *IU Health*, Indiana University Health, 8 Mar. 2022, https://iuhealth.org/thrive/is-addiction-really-a-disease#:~:text=The%20American%20Medical%20Association%20(AMA,result%20of%20making%20bad%20choices.

15 *Alcoholics Anonymous: The Story of How More than One Hundred Men Have Recovered from Alcoholism.* Literary Licensing, 2020.

16 "Dual Diagnosis." *Alcohol Rehab Guide*, 21 Sept. 2022, https://www.alcoholrehabguide.org/resources/dual-diagnosis/.

17 "Co-Occurring Disorders and Other Health Conditions." *SAMHSA*, U.S. Department of Health & Human Services, 27 June 2022, https://www.samhsa.gov/medication-assisted-treatment/medications-counseling-related-conditions/co-occurring-disorders.

18 Gibson, R M, and D R Waldo. "National Health Expenditures, 1980." *Health Care Financing Review*, CENTERS for MEDICARE & MEDICAID SERVICES, Sept. 1981, https://www.ncbi.nlm.nih.gov/pmc/articles/PMC4191238/.

19 "Historical." *CMS*, 15 Dec. 2021, https://www.cms.gov/Research-Statistics-Data-and-Systems/Statistics-Trends-and-Reports/NationalHealthExpendData/NationalHealthAccountsHistorical.

20 "Reducing the Economic Burden of Unmet Mental Health Needs." *The White House*, The United States Government, 17 June 2022, https://www.whitehouse.gov/cea/written-materials/2022/05/31/reducing-the-economic-burden-of-unmet-mental-health-needs/.

21 "2019 U.S. Mental Health Spending Topped $225 Billion, with per Capita Spending Ranging from $37 in Florida to $375 in Maine – Open Minds Releases New Analysis." *OPEN MINDS*, 10 May 2020, https://openminds.com/press/u-s-mental-health-spending-reached-225-1-billion-in-2019-open-minds-releases-new-analysis-on-market-spending/.

22 "Nhe Fact Sheet." *CMS*, 12 Aug. 2022, https://www.cms.gov/Research-Statistics-Data-and-Systems/Statistics-Trends-and-Reports/NationalHealthExpendData/NHE-Fact-Sheet.

23 "Statistics." *National Institute of Mental Health*, U.S. Department of Health and Human Services, https://www.nimh.nih.gov/health/statistics.

24 "Suicide." *National Institute of Mental Health*, U.S. Department of Health and Human Services, https://www.nimh.nih.gov/health/statistics/suicide.

CPSIA information can be obtained
at www.ICGtesting.com
Printed in the USA
LVHW021407100523
746592LV00009B/580